The mortal remains of former Prime Minister Atal Bihari Vajpayee being taken to Smriti Sthal for the funeral. Prime Minister Narendra Modi, BJP President Amit Shah and other BJP leaders accompanied the procession along with lakhs of his admirers.

President Ram Nath Kovind saluting the departed soul after laying wreath on the body of Prime Minister Atal Bihari Vajpayee.

Prime Minister Narendra Modi paying homage to the departed sou after laying wreath on the body of Prime Minister Atal Bihar Vajpayee.

President Pranab Mukherjee conferring the Bharat Ratna on Atal Bihari Vajpayee at a special function at his residence in New Delhi, 27th March 2015.

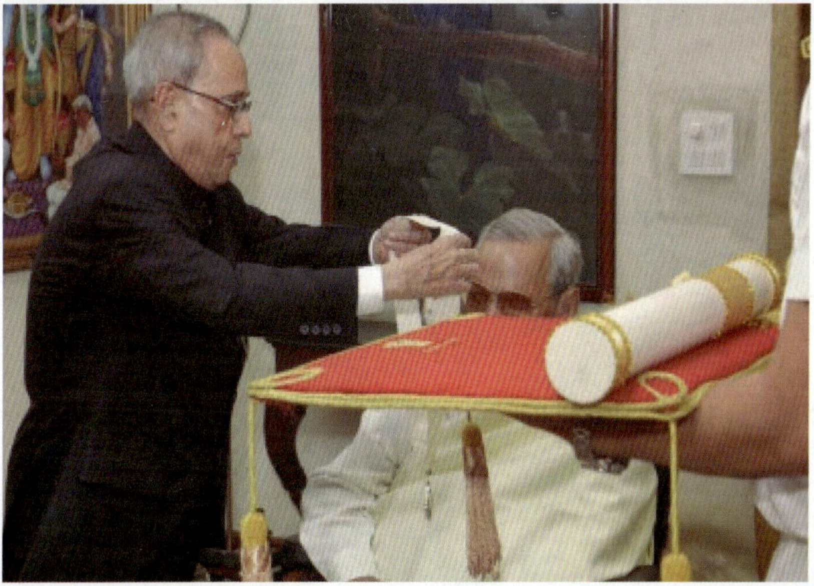

Prime Minister Atal Bihari Vajpayee at the site of the nuclear test at Pokhran in May 1998. Also seen is DRDO chief APJ Abdul Kalam.

Prime Minister Atal Bihari Vajpayee shake hands with Pakistan Prime Minister Nawaz Sharif during his visit to Pakistan to sign the Lahore Treaty, 21st February 1999.

President KR Narayanan administering the oath of office to Prime Minister Atal Bihari Vajpayee on 13th October 1999.

US President Bill Clinton and First Lady Hillary Clinton welcome PM Atal Bihari Vajpayee, White House, 16th September 2000.

Russian President Vladimir Putin held talks with Prime Minister Atal Bihari Vajpayee at New Delhi, 3rd October 2000.

Prime Minister Atal Bihari Vajpayee welcomed by Malaysian Prime Minister Mahathir Mohamad, 14th May 2001.

American President George W Bush welcomes Prime Minister o India Atal Bihari Vajpayee to the Oval Office, 9th November 2001.

British Prime Minister Tony Blair meets Prime Minister Atal Bihar Vajpayee during his visit to London, 12th November 2001.

Prime Minister Atal Bihari Vajpayee with President APJ Abdu Kalam.

Prime Minister Atal Bihari Vajpayee delivering speech at Unitec Nations General Assembly, 13th September 2002.

Prime Minister Atal Bihari Vajpayee with Bangladesh Prime Minister Sheikh Hasina in New Delhi, 26th November 2002.

Atal Bihari Vajpayee with Sri Lankan President Chandrika Kumaratunga in New Delhi on 10th April 2003.

Prime Minister Atal Bihari Vajpayee greeted by Chinese President Hu Jintao at the Great Hall of the People in Beijing, China, 24th June 2003.

Prime Minister Atal Bihari Vajpayee delivering speech from Red Fort. 15th August 1999.

Israeli Prime Minster Ariel Sharon shakes hands with Indian Prime Minister Atal Bihari Vajpayee, 9th September 2003.

PM Atal Bihari Vajpayee shaking hands with Indonesian President Megawati Sukarnoputri in Nusa Dua, Bali, 8th October 2003.

ormer Prime Minister of Pakistan Ms Benazir Bhutto calls on the Prime Minister Atal Bihari Vajpayee, 12th Dec 2003, New Delhi.

Narendra Modi, Chief Minister of Gujarat meets Prime Minister Atal Bihari Vajpayee, 10th January 2003.

Prime Minister Atal Bihari Vajpayee, Vice-President Bhairon Singh Shekhawat and Deputy Prime Minister Lal Krishna Advani.

Prime Minister Atal Bihari Vajpayee with Lal Krishna Advani and Arun Jaitley.

Sushma Swaraj, Minister of Health and Family Welfare, Venkaiah Naidu, Minister of Rural Development with PM Vajpayee.

Shiv Sena Chief Bal Thakrey with Prime Minister Vajpayee.

Former Prime Minister Atal Bihari Vajpayee lighting the inaugura
amp of BJP's National Executive Meeting with Rajnath Singh, LK
Advani and Dr Harsh Vardhan, New Delhi, 25 June 2006.

Prime Minister Vajpayee with Vijay Goel, Union Minister of State
PMO and Statistics & Programme Implementation.

Prime Minister Atal Bihari Vajpayee with Shivraj Singh Chauhan and Ananth Kumar.

Foreign Minister Atal Bihari Vajpayee delivering his first speech in Hindi at United Nations, 4th October 1977.

Poet
to
Prime Minister

Atal Bihari Vajpayee

Poet
to
Prime Minister
Atal Bihari Vajpayee

Vivek Garg
(Advocate & RTI Activist)

Manas Publications
(We Convert Fighters into Writers)
New Delhi - 110 002 (INDIA)

MANAS PUBLICATIONS
(We Convert Fighters into Writers)
(Publishers, Library Suppliers, Importers & Exporters)
4402/5-A, Ansari Road (Opp. HDFC Bank)
Darya Ganj, New Delhi - 110 002 (India)
Phones: Off.: 011-23260783, 23265523, Res.: 011-23842660
E-mail: manaspublications@gmail.com
manaspublications@yahoo.com
Website: www.manaspublications.in

ISBN 978-81-7049-551-2
₹ 795

Designed by
Veronica Grafic Arts

Printed in India at
R.K. Print Services, Delhi

Published by Mrs Suman Lata for
Manas Publications
4402/5-A, Ansari Road (Opp HDFC Bank),
Darya Ganj, New Delhi - 110002 (INDIA)

Contents

Introduction

Bharat Ratna Atal Bihari Vajpayee, former Prime Minister, an orator, poet, politician, an impeccable parliamentarian for over five decades, was undergoing treatment at the All India Institute of Medical Sciences, New Delhi, breathed his last at 5:05 PM on 16th August 2018. Political leaders cutting across partly lines thronged the hospital to enquire about Vajpayee's health. Making his second visit to AIIMS in less than 24 hours, Prime Minister Narendra Modi visited the AIIMS to enquire about the health of former Prime Minister Atal Bihari Vajpayee. He was suffering from kidney tract infection, urinary tract infection, low urine output and chest congestion.

The glass coffin, draped in India's flag was followed by Prime Minister Narendra Modi with many of his cabinet members and BJP President Amit Shah on foot from the BJP headquarters to Smriti Sthal along with lakhs of admirers. Never before any Prime Minister walked 6 kilometres like this in a public procession. A huge crowd of people showered petals at the funeral procession and jostled to get a glimpse of the former Prime Minister. A seven-day state mourning was announced by the Government of India.

Thousands of people, including political leaders and foreign dignitaries paid their last tributes to former Prime

Minister Atal Bihari Vajpayee during his funeral at Rashtriya Smriti Sthal, adjoining Rajghat, New Delhi.

President Ram Nath Kovind, Vice-President Venkaiah Naidu, Prime Minister Narendra Modi, BJP Chief Amit Shah, senior BJP leaders LK Advani and MM Joshi, Union Ministers, Congress President Rahul Gandhi and former Prime Minister Dr Manmohan Singh and other dignitaries were present at Smriti Sthal on the banks of river Yamuna.

Several Chief Ministers, including Delhi's Arvind Kejriwal and Chhattisgarh's Raman Singh, and Congress leaders Ghulam Nabi Azad, Anand Sharma, Ashok Gehlot and Raj Babbar were also present at the funeral.

Foreign dignitaries, including King of Bhutan Jigme Khesar Namgyel Wangchuk and Nepal's Minister for Foreign Affairs Pradeep Kumar Gyawali, laid a wreath to honour one of India's tallest leaders. Sri Lanka's Acting Foreign Minister Lakshman Kiriella and former Afghanistan President Hamid Karzai also attended the funeral.

The Chiefs of Indian Army, Indian Navy and Indian Air Force saluted the leader and laid wreaths on his body. President Ram Nath Kovind, Prime Minister Narendra Modi and many other dignitaries also laid wreaths on the body of former Prime Minister Atal Bihari Vajpayee.

Last rites of Vajpayee were performed by his adopted daughter Namita Bhattacharya. His daughter lighted the funeral pyre and the former Prime Minister was laid to rest with full state honours. August 17, 2018, marks the end of an era and the entire country pays adieu to the remarkable leader. The ashes of former Prime Minister Atal Bihari Vajpayee were immersed in the river Ganga at Har-ki-Pauri in Haridwar on 19th August by his family members amidst chanting of Vedic hymns. His ashes were also immersed in about 100 rivers spread over 29 states and 7 Union Territories, as he was very much attached to the rivers and wanted to unite and integrate the masses of the country through rivers.

A member of the Bharatiya Janata Party, Atal Bihari Vajpayee is also known for his great oratory skills. Apart from being a politician, he was also an acclaimed writer who has written various poems. As a student leader he had joined the Quit India Movement in 1942. He was awarded highest civilian honour 'Bharat Ratna' in 2015 on his birthday. His birthday, 25 December, was also declared as 'Good Governance Day' by the Narendra Modi government. He was also a member of the Rashtriya Swayamsevak Sangh and worked as a journalist for a short period before he joined BJP. He credited RSS Pracharak Narayanrao Tarte for shaping his ideology for the development of the country. He wrote his famous poem 'Hindu Tan-man Hindu Jeevan' in class X in 1947 and decided to give up studies to become a whole-time volunteer of the RSS. He was the first non-Congress political leader who became the Prime Minister of India. He went to jail when the Emergency was declared by Indira Gandhi government in June 1975.

Atal Bihari Vajpayee was born to Krishna Devi and Krishna Bihari Vajpayee on 25 December 1924 in Gwalior. His grandfather, Pandit Shyam Lal Vajpayee, had migrated to Morena, Gwalior from his ancestral village of Bateshwar, Uttar Pradesh. His father, Krishna Bihari Vajpayee, was a school teacher. He did his schooling from the Saraswati Shishu Mandir, Gwalior. Subsequently he attended Gwalior's Victoria College (now Laxmi Bai College) and graduated with distinction in Hindi, English and Sanskrit. He completed his post-graduation in Political Science from DAV College, Kanpur, and was awarded a first-class degree.

His activism started with Arya Kumar Sabha of Gwalior, the youth wing of the Arya Samaj, of which he became the General Secretary in 1944. He also joined the Rashtriya Swayamsevak Sangh (RSS) as a Swayamsevak in 1939. Influenced by Babasaheb Apte, he attended the Officers Training Camp of the RSS during 1940-44 and became a

Pracharak in 1947. He gave up studying law due to the partition riots. He was sent as a Vistarak, a probationary Pracharak, to Uttar Pradesh and quickly began working for the newspapers of Deendayal Upadhyaya, *Rashtradharma* (Hindi monthly), *Panchjanya* (Hindi weekly) and the dailies *Swadesh* and *Veer Arjun*.

By 1942, Atal Bihari Vajpayee, though only 16 years old at that time, had already become an active member of the Rashtriya Swayamsevak Sangh. In August 1942, he and his elder brother Prem were arrested for 24 days during the Quit India Movement.

In 1948, RSS was banned for its alleged role in the assassination of Mahatma Gandhi. In 1951, he was seconded by the RSS, along with Deendayal Upadhyaya, to work for the newly formed Bharatiya Jana Sangh. He was appointed as a National Secretary of the party in charge of the Northern region, based in Delhi. He soon became a follower and aide of party leader Syama Prasad Mookerjee. In 1954, Vajpayee was with Mookerjee when he went on a fast-unto-death in Kashmir to protest against the perceived inferior treatment of non-Kashmiri visitors to the State. Mookerjee died in prison during this strike. In 1957, Vajpayee lost to Raja Mahendra Pratap in Mathura for the Lok Sabha, but was elected from Balrampur. There, his oratorial skills so impressed Prime Minister Jawaharlal Nehru that he predicted that Atal Bihari Vajpayee would someday become the Prime Minister of India.

Atal Bihari Vajpayee's oratorial skills led him to acquire the reputation of being the most eloquent defender of the Jana Sangh's policies. After the death of Deendayal Upadhyaya, Vajpayee was appointed the leader of Jana Sangh. He became the National President of Jana Sangh in 1968, running the party along with Nanaji Deshmukh, Balraj Madhok and LK Advani.

In 1975, Atal Bihari Vajpayee was arrested along with several opposition leaders during the Internal Emergency imposed by the then Prime Minister Mrs Indira Gandhi.

The opposition leaders were tortured badly during the Emergency period.

A coalition of parties, called the Janata Party, won the 1977 general elections. Morarji Desai, leader of the alliance, became the Prime Minister. Atal Bihari Vajpayee was appointed as the Minister of External Affairs. As Foreign Minister, Vajpayee became the first person in 1977 to deliver a speech in the United Nations General Assembly in Hindi. By the time Janata government crumbled in 1979, Vajpayee had established himself as an experienced statesman and a respected political leader.

Janata Party was dissolved soon after Morarji Desai resigned as Prime Minister in 1979. Jana Sangh had devoted its political organisation to sustain the coalition and was left exhausted by the internecine political wars within the Janata Party.

In 1980, Atal Bihari Vajpayee joined many of his Bharatiya Jana Sangh and Rashtriya Swayamsevak Sangh colleagues, particularly his long-time friends LK Advani and Bhairon Singh Shekhawat, to form the Bharatiya Janata Party (BJP). He became the first President of BJP. He emerged as a strong critic of Congress government that followed the Janata government.

While the BJP opposed the Sikh militancy that was rising in the State of Punjab, it also blamed Prime Minister Indira Gandhi for her "divisive and corrupt politics that fostered such militancy at the expense of national unity and integrity." The BJP was left with only two parliamentary seats in the 1984 elections. During this period, Atal Bihari Vajpayee remained at the centre-stage as party President and Leader of the Opposition in the Parliament.

BJP became the political voice of the Ram Janmabhoomi Mandir Movement, which was led by activists of the Vishva Hindu Parishad (VHP) and the RSS, and which sought to build a temple dedicated to Lord Rama in Ayodhya.

Victory in the assembly elections of Gujarat and Maharashtra in March 1995, and a good performance in the elections to the Karnataka assembly in December 1994, propelled the BJP to greater political prominence. During a BJP conference in Mumbai in November 1995, BJP President LK Advani declared that Atal Bihari Vajpayee would become the Prime Minister of India.

BJP grew in strength in the early 1995, riding on nationalist sentiment in the country. In the 1996 general elections, the BJP emerged as the single largest party in the Lok Sabha. The then President Shankar Dayal Sharma invited Vajpayee to form the government. Vajpayee was sworn in as the 10th Prime Minister of India, but the BJP failed to muster enough support from other parties to obtain a majority. He resigned after 13 days when it became clear that he could not garner a majority.

After the fall of the two United Front governments between 1996 and 1998, Lok Sabha was dissolved and fresh elections were held. The 1998 general elections again put the BJP ahead of others. This time, a cohesive bloc of political parties joined the BJP to form the National Democratic Alliance (NDA), and Vajpayee was sworn in as the Prime Minister.

NDA proved its majority in the parliament. The government lasted 13 months until mid-1999 when the All India Anna Dravida Munnetra Kazhagam (AIADMK) under Jayalalithaa withdrew its support to the government. The government lost the ensuing vote of confidence motion in the Lok Sabha by a single vote on 17 April 1999. As the Opposition was unable to come up with the numbers to form the new government, once again Lok Sabha was dissolved and fresh elections were held. Vajpayee remained the Prime Minister until the elections were held.

The Vajpayee-led government was faced with two crises in mid-1999. The AIADMK had continually threatened to withdraw from the coalition and national leaders repeatedly flew down from Delhi to Chennai to pacify the AIADMK chief J Jayalalithaa. However, in May 1999, the AIADMK did pull the plug on the NDA, and the Vajpayee administration was reduced to a caretaker status pending fresh elections scheduled for October 1999.

General Elections were held from 5 September to 3 October 1999, a few months after the Kargil War. The 13th Lok Sabha election is of historical importance as it was the first time a united front of parties managed to attain a majority and form a government that lasted a full term of five years, thus ending a period of political instability at the national level that had been characterised by three general elections held in as many years.

As the first non-Congress Prime Minister to complete five years, Vajpayee's Premiership was as significant as it was eventful.

Operation Shakti – Pokhran-II

Under Prime Minister Atal Bihari Vajpayee's government, India gained the status of 'full-fledged nuclear state'. Pokhran-II was the second Indian nuclear test, the first being 'Operation Smiling Buddha' conducted in May 1974. Pokhran-II was a series of five nuclear bomb test explosions conducted by the Indian Army at the Pokhran Test Range (PTR), located in Rajasthan's Jaisalmer district in May 1998. The test consisted of five detonations, the first was a fusion bomb while the remaining four were fission bombs. The project was titled 'Operation Shakti'; and on 11th May 1998, the project was initiated with the detonation of one fusion and two fission bombs. Subsequently, on 13th May 1998, two more fission bombs were detonated. A variety of sanctions were levied on India by a number of major countries. While some nations, such as Russia and France, endorsed India's right to defensive nuclear power, others including the United States, Canada, Japan, Britain and the European Union imposed sanctions on information, resources and technology to India. In spite of intense international criticism and steady decline in foreign investment and trade, the nuclear tests were popular domestically. In effect, the international sanctions imposed failed to sway India from weaponising its nuclear capability. US sanctions against India and Pakistan were eventually lifted after just six months, a development that the Vajpayee administration had anticipated and planned for.

Gujarat Earthquake, 2001

A 7.7 earthquake hit southwest Gujarat on 26 January 2001. The disaster killed nearly 20,000 individuals, injured 1,67,000 and caused massive infrastructure and economic damage. The Indian Army led relief efforts and the Government called for $ 1.5 billion in international loans to deal with the devastation.

Foreign Policy

In the post-Cold War world, Vajpayee boosted trade and bilateral relations with the United States. In 2000, Bill Clinton became the first American President to visit India since Jimmy Carter's visit in 1978. Vajpayee also championed a diplomatic solution to the land disputes between India and China.

Foreign Policy Regarding Pakistan

Vajpayee's greatest foreign policy efforts lay in his approach to Pakistan. On 19 February 1999, he inaugurated the Delhi-Lahore bus service by travelling in the same to meet his counterpart Nawaz Sharif in Pakistan. This incident became an iconic symbol of international diplomacy and Vajpayee was lauded globally for his pragmatism. The two Prime Ministers agreed on a historic treaty on 21 February 1999 called the Lahore Declaration. The Declaration put forth common goals of peace and bilateral friendship between the two countries and had several contents including nuclear non-proliferation and increased trade relations. However, for all its hype and promise, the Lahore Declaration fell flat after the Kargil War began in May 1999. Hope for a diplomatic solution rose during the Agra Summit between Vajpayee and Pakistani President Pervez Musharraf in July 2001. The Summit failed to transpire into action. After two successive attacks on Indian sovereignty - first on the J&K Legislative Assembly and then the Parliament - the 2001-2002 India-Pakistan military standoff brought the two nuclear weapon States dangerously close to war.

Economy

Building upon 1991 economic reforms, Vajpayee government privatised many State-controlled institutions. It was only Atal Bihari Vajpayee, leader of a complex coalition, who championed the cause of minimum government and made sure that the government has no business in doing business. He successfully implemented a privatisation policy, and with the sale of 28 companies, his government showed that running hotels or making bread is not where government should meddle.

The Vajpayee government saw significant expansion in India's economy. Between 1999 and 2004, when the BJP-led NDA government was in power under Atal Bihari Vajpayee, the average GDP growth rate was at 6% per year. However, upon leaving the office, the GDP rate was recorded at 8% under the Vajpayee government. The rate of inflation at this period was at 4.8% but remained relatively stable at that number.

Fiscal Responsibility Act 2003

Prime Minister Vajpayee's government introduced the Fiscal Responsibility and Budget Management Bill (FRBM) to eliminate revenue deficit. The Bill raised the concern in regards to the terrible state of government finances in India, both at the Union and the state levels. It also sought to introduce the concept of 'fiscal discipline' at various levels of the government. The Bill was approved by the Union government's Cabinet in February 2003. Following due exactment process in the Parliament, it was approved by President of India on 26th August 2003. The Bill became effective on 5th July 2004.

Asset Reconstruction Companies (ARC)

In a bid to eliminate failing Public Sector Undertakings, Vajpayee government introduced the Securitisation and Reconstruction of Financial Assets and Enforcement of Security Interest (SARFAESI) Act, 2002; enacted in December 2002. The total worth of non-performing assets (NPA) ratios crossed 10%. The Act was introduced with the aim of reconstructing bad assets without the intervention of courts. Since then, a large number of Asset Reconstruction Companies (ARC) were formed and registered with the Reserve Bank of India (RBI) which also became the regulatory authority for the ARCs. An Asset Reconstruction Company is a specialised financial institution that buys the NPAs or bad assets from banks and financial institutions in a bid to help them clean up their balance sheets. This helps the banks to concentrate on normal banking activities. Rather than going after defaulters, banks can sell bad assets to the ARCs at a mutually agreed value.

Privatisation

Department of Disinvestments was created by the Vajpayee government to process privatisation of government-owned companies, along with the creation of a Cabinet Committee on Disinvestment for regulating expeditious approvals. Vajpayee government's drive towards privatisation began with the sale of Modern Food Industries to Hindustan Unilever (HUL) in 2000. Following this, his government facilitated the sale of Bharat Aluminium Company Ltd (BALCO) and Hindustan Zinc Ltd to Anil Agarwal's Sterlite Industries. The IT companies, CMC Ltd and Videsh Sanchar Nigam Ltd (VSNL), were sold to Tata. Fuel retailers IBP Co Ltd was sold to Indian Oil Corporation (IOC) and Indian Petrochemicals Corporation Ltd (IPCL).

Sarva Shiksha Abhiyan

Sarva Shiksha Abhiyan (SSA) is a programme for Universal Elementary Education. This programme is mandated by the 86th Amendment to the Constitution of India, making free and compulsory education to children between the ages of 6 and 14, a fundamental right. The programme is an attempt at providing opportunities for improving human capabilities to all children through provision of community-owned quality education in a mission mode. The objectives of this programme are:

- to provide useful and elementary education to all children from ages 6 to 14,
- to bridge social, regional and gender gaps, to foster active participation of community in the management of schools,
- to allow children to learn about their natural environment in order to develop material and spiritual potential, and
- to inculcate a value-based learning system, and to realise the importance of early childhood care with ages 0 to 14 being the continuum.

Infrastructure Developments

In what was the continuation of economic policies, the Vajpayee government also facilitated the growth of infrastructure in India. Prime Minister Vajpayee's main focus was on building connectivity through road networks throughout India.

His government was responsible to building India's most famous highway project, the National Highways Development Project (NHDP) to connect the major metropolitan cities of India and to increase employment and bolster infrastructure. The government under Vajpayee also launched the Pradhan Mantri Gramin Sadak Yojana (PMGSY), a scheme launched to build roads in villages and provide connectivity between them. The government encouraged foreign investment and approved the Delhi Metro Project. Indeed, the fact that Vajpayee maintained steady economic growth at 6-8% in spite of natural disasters, the Gulf War, the oil crises, 9/11 attack, the War on Terror, the Kargil War and the Indo-Pak military standoff, all are applaudable achievements.

National Highways Development Project (NHDP)

The National Highways Development Project (NHDP) project is managed by the National Highways Authority of India (NHAI) and the Ministry of Road, Transport and Highways. This project represents 49,260 kilometres of roads and highway networks, to boost economic development of the country.

Phase I of NHDP is known as the Golden Quadrilateral, spanning 5,846 kilometres, connecting the four major cities of Delhi, Mumbai, Chennai and Kolkata. The four-lane GQ highway was declared complete in January 2012.

Phase II comprised of highway networks connecting the North-South and East-West corridors; connecting the four extreme points of the country. The project's total length is 7,142 kilometres, connecting Srinagar in the north to Kanyakumari in the south, and Silchar in the east to Porbandar in the west. As of October 2016, 90.99% of the project had been completed; 3.52% of the total length is to be finished while 5.47% is under implementation.

Pradhan Mantri Gramin Sadak Yojana (PMGSY)

The Pradhan Mantri Gram Sadak Yojana (PMGSY) is a centrally sponsored scheme that was introduced in 2000 by the BJP-led NDA government under Prime Minister Atal Bihari Vajpayee. The scheme is a nationwide plan to provide effective, all-weather road connectivity to, and between, villages. The PMGSY is under the authority of the Ministry of Rural Development, and work began on 25th December 2000. As of December 2017; 82% of about 1.7 lakh villages with a population above 500 in the plains and 250 in hilly areas, were connected.

New Telecom Policy

In 1999, Prime Minister Atal Bihari Vajpayee's government launched the New Telecom Policy on the basis of a report by a group on telecommunications. A high-level Group on Telecommunications (GoT) was constituted by the government to review the then existing National Telecom Policy of 1994. The reason for the enactment of the new policy was the fact that the goals of the existing policy of 1994 were not achieved within the stipulated time period, while immense growth was being recorded in information and communication technology. Under the New Telecom Policy of 1999, the objectives were:

- to provide affordable and effective means of telecommunications for all citizens,
- to encourage the development of telecommunication facilities in remote, hilly and tribal areas of the country,
- to form modern and efficient telecommunications systems based on the IT convergence with media and consumer electronics, and
- to strike a balance in providing universal services to all uncovered areas with the help of high level services.

Lahore Declaration

Period after the 1971 Indo-Pakistan War was characterised by long periods of relatively few armed conflicts involving the armies of India and Pakistan. During the 1990s, there were escalating tensions between the two nations due to separatist activities in Kashmir, some perpetrated by Pakistan. The conducting of nuclear tests by both countries in 1998, led to an increasingly fragile atmosphere. In a bid to diffuse the situation, India and Pakistan signed the Lahore Declaration in February 1999.

The Lahore Declaration was a bilateral agreement and governance treaty signed on 21st February 1999, at the conclusion of a historic summit in Lahore. The summit was consented to, by the parliaments of both the nations. The terms of the treaty called for reaching a mutual understanding in regards to development of atomic arsenals and to avoid accidental and/or unauthorised use of nuclear weapons. The treaty was signed by Pakistani Prime Minister Nawaz Sharif and Prime Minister Atal Bihari Vajpayee, in a widely-covered televised press conference in both countries.

Operation Vijay – Kargil War

In a move that almost marred the progress presumably achieved by the Lahore Declaration, Pakistani soldiers infiltrated the Indian border disguised at Kashmiri militants and assimilated themselves into positions on the Indian side of the Line of Control (LoC). The armed conflict is a significant example of high-altitude warfare in mountainous terrain. It is also an example of the direct confrontation of armed forced between nuclear states.

During the initial stages of the War, Pakistan completely deflected blame towards Kashmiri insurgents. However, documents left behind by casualties and later statements made by Prime Minister Nawaz Sharif suggested the involvement of Pakistani paramilitary forces, led by General Ashraf Rashid.

India managed to recapture a majority of its position on the Indian side of the LoC infiltrated by Pakistani troops and militants, with the help of the Indian Army and the Indian Air Force. On 11 July, after extensive fighting, and on being prompted by the US to withdraw its troops from the remaining Indian positions along the LoC, Pakistan withdrew its troops from the area completely. The casualties accounted for 527 Indian soldiers being killed, while 1,363 soldiers were wounded.

The Kargil War came at a time when India witnessed the explosive growth of electronic journalism. News stories on the Kargil War, as well as footages were telecast on live television, while many websites provided an in-depth analysis of the events. The conflict became the first 'live' war in South Asia.

Aadhaar

The idea of Aadhaar was first mooted after the Kargil War. According to the Unique Identification Authority of India (UIDAI), a report with a proposal for citizens in border regions to be issued identity cards was submitted to Prime Minister Vajpayee. A group of ministers led by LK Advani accepted the recommendation. Later the Ministry of External Affairs proposed that a national identity be issued.

Indian Airlines Hijack

On 24 December 1999, Indian Airlines Flight IC-814 was hijacked by five terrorists and flown to Taliban-ruled Afghanistan. The hijackers demanded the release of certain terrorists held in India. The seven-day-long hostage crisis ended after India agreed to release three militants in exchange of the passengers.

Chandrayaan-I

On 15th August 2003, the then Prime Minister Atal Bihari Vajpayee announced 'Chandrayaan-I' as part of his Independence Day address. The idea of a scientific mission to the moon was first pitched in 1999, during a meeting at the Indian Academy of Sciences. The idea was carried forward in 2000, by the Astronomical Society of India. Soon after, the Indian Space Research Organisation (ISRO) set up the National Lunar Mission Task Force. Over a hundred scientists from various fields of planetary and space sciences, met in April 2003, and discussed and approved the Task Force recommendation to launch an Indian probe to the moon. The mission was approved by the Indian government in November 2003.

Chandrayaan-I was the first lunar probe, designed and launched by India. The probe was launched by ISRO in October 2008, and operated until August 2009. The mission included a lunar orbiter and an impactor. India launched the spacecraft on 22nd October 2008 from the Satish Dhawan Space Centre, located about 80 kms from Chennai. The vehicle was inserted into orbit on 8th November 2008. The mission was a major boost to India's space programme. India also became the fourth country to place its flag on the moon.

Fundamental Political Reforms

Atalji took bold steps to bring about fundamental reforms, whether in our election process or about the shortcomings concerning the people's representatives. On the basis of his initiatives for changing the political culture of the country, presently efforts are afoot and discussions are being held about simultaneously holding the elections for Lok Sabha and for state assemblies.

For good governance, Vajpayee brought up the 91st Amendment Act, 2003, that restricted the size of the Cabinet in states to 15% of the total seats in the state assembly. He was instrumental in increasing the limit under the anti-defection law from one-thirds to two-thirds of the members of a party. The amendment to the anti-defection law resulted in defining clear guidelines to disqualify the defector.

For many years in India, the political culture of forming a very large Cabinet was being misused to constitute jumbo cabinets not only to create a divide, but also to appease political leaders. Atalji changed it. The effort resulted in saving of money and resources besides improving efficiency.

Timeline

1924: Born to Krishna Devi and Krishna Bihari Vajpayee on 25 December in Gwalior.

1942: Participated in the Quit India Movement and was arrested with his brother for 23 days.

1942: Sangh Pracharak.

1951: Started working for Bharatiya Jana Sangh, a political wing of RSS.

1957: The year was a landmark in Vajpayee's career, as it marked his entry into the mainstream politics. In the Lok Sabha Elections, he won from Balrampur and became a Member of Parliament.

1962: Elected to a six-year term in the Rajya Sabha.

1968: After the death of Jana Sangh co-founder Deendayal Upadhyaya in a train accident, Vajpayee took over the reins of the party and became the National President of the party.

1975: Arrested along with opposition leaders during the Emergency period imposed by the then Prime Minister Indira Gandhi.

1977: After the emergency was withdrawn, Jana Sangh merged with other opposition parties to form Janata Party, solely to oppose the rule of Indian National Congress. In the general elections that year, Janata Party emerged as the victor and formed government led by Morarji Desai as Prime Minister. Vajpayee became the Minister for External Affairs in his cabinet.

1977: Delivered speech in Hindi in United Nations on 4th October.

1980: Janata Party dissolved after Morarji Desai resigned as Prime Minister. Vajpayee joined LK Advani, Bhairon Singh Shekhawat and other RSS, Jana Sangh colleagues to form Bharatiya Janata Party (BJP) and became the party's first President.

1984: In the coming years, the party struggled and in fact in 1984 elections, BJP was left with only two seats in the Parliament. Vajpayee led the party during these years and supported the Ram Janmabhoomi Mandir Movement by RSS and Vishva Hindu Parishad (VHP).

1992: Awarded Padma Vibhushan.

1993: Made Leader of Opposition in Lok Sabha.

1994: BJP came into prominence again after a good performance in Karnataka Assembly Elections in 1994. The party won 40 seats out of 224 seats in the polls. Later in 1995, in Maharashtra and Gujarat assembly elections, the party again showed a good performance and won 65 seats and 121 seats in the states. This brought back Vajpayee and BJP into political centre stage in the country.

1996: In the general elections this year, BJP had the majority winning 161 seats and Vajpayee became the Prime Minister of India. However, the party was unable to get support from other parties to get more than 200 seats to form the government and therefore resigned after 13 days.

1998: BJP came back into power in 1998. The National Democratic Alliance (NDA) was formed and Vajpayee became the Prime Minister again.

1998: Pokhran atomic test done successfully in May.

1999: Bus journey to Lahore on 19th February.

1999: Won the Kargil War.

1999: His government was dissolved after Jayalalithaa-led AIADMK withdrew its support after 13 months and the government came down.

1999: Resigns after his government loses a parliamentary vote of confidence on 17 April.

1999: Sworn in again as Prime Minister after his party and its allies regained control on 13th October.

2000: Along with US President Bill Clinton, Vajpayee signs a statement on "US-India Relations: A Vision for the 21st Century," while hosting him in New Delhi. The document proposes many new endeavours, including a "pledge to reduce impediments to bilateral trade and investment, and to expand commerce between the two nations."

2000: On 14th September, Vajpayee addresses the joint session of the US Congress where he states that his visit to the US has "consolidated relations between the world's two largest democracies and marked a new era in bilateral and global affairs."

2001: National Highway Project, encouraging private sector and foreign investments, reducing the minimum government holding in PSBs, introduction of Asset Reconstruction Companies - were introduced.

2004: The 13th Lok Sabha had been dissolved before the full-term as the BJP was confident that it would come back to power again. However, the party witnessed a crushing defeat.

2005: Announces his retirement from politics.

2009: In February, hospitalized with a respiratory infection and was put on a ventilator.

2009: On 1 March released from the hospital.

2014: 25 December, Vajpayee's 90th birthday is being observed nationally as Good Governance Day.

2015: On 27th March, India's highest civilian honour 'Bharat Ratna' was conferred upon Vajpayee by the then President Pranab Mukherjee.

2018: Left for heavenly abode on 16th August.

यू एन में तत्कालीन विदेश मंत्री श्री अटल बिहारी वाजपेयी का हिंदी में भाषण (4 अक्टूबर 1977)

मैं भारत की जनता की ओर से राष्ट्र संघ के लिए शुभकामनाओं का संदेश लाया हूँ। महासभा के इस 32वें अधिवेशन के अवसर पर मैं राष्ट्र संघ में भारत की दृढ़ आस्था को पुनः व्यक्त करना चाहता हूँ। जनता सरकार को शासन की बागडोर संभाले केवल छह मास हुए हैं। फिर भी इतने अल्प समय में हमारी उपलब्धियाँ उल्लेखनीय हैं। भारत में मूलभूत मानव अधिकार पुनः प्रतिष्ठित हो गए हैं। जिस भय और आतंक के वातावरण ने हमारे लोगों को घेर लिया था वह दूर हो गया है। ऐसे संवैधानिक कदम उठाए जा रहे हैं जिनसे यह सुनिश्चित हो जाए कि लोकतंत्र और बुनियादी आजादी का अब फिर कभी हनन नहीं होगा।

अध्यक्ष महोदय, "वसुधैव कुटुंबकम" की परिकल्पना बहुत पुरानी है। भारत में सदा से हमारा इस धारणा में विश्वास रहा है कि सारा संसार एक परिवार है। अनेकानेक प्रयत्नों और कष्टों के बाद संयुक्त राष्ट्र के रूप में इस स्वप्न के अब साकार होने की संभावना है।

यहाँ मैं राष्ट्रों की सत्ता और महत्ता के बारे में नहीं सोच रहा हूँ, आम आदमी की प्रतिष्ठा और प्रगति मेरे लिए कहीं अधिक महत्व रखती है। अंततः हमारी सफलताएं और असफलताएं केवल एक ही मापदंड से मापी जानी चाहिए कि क्या हम पूरे मानव समाज वस्तुतः हर नर, नारी और बालक के लिए न्याय और गरिमा की आश्वस्ती देने में प्रयत्नशील हैं। अफ्रीका में चुनौती स्पष्ट है। प्रश्न यह है कि किसी जनता को स्वतंत्रता और सम्मान के साथ रहने का अनपरणीय अधिकार है या रंगभेद में विश्वास रखने वाला अल्पमत किसी विशाल बहुमत पर हमेशा अन्याय और दमन करता रहेगा। निःसंदेह रंगभेद के सभी रूपों का जड़ से उन्मूलन होना चाहिए।

हाल में इजराइल ने वेस्ट बैंक और गाजा में नयी बस्तियां बसाकर अधिकृत क्षेत्रों में जनसंख्या परिवर्तन करने का जो प्रयत्न किया है संयुक्त राष्ट्र को उसे पूरी तरह अस्वीकार और रद्द कर देना चाहिए। यदि इन समस्याओं का संतोषजनक और शीघ्र ही समाधान नहीं होता तो इसके दुष्परिणाम इस क्षेत्र के बाहर भी फैल सकते हैं। यह अति आवश्यक है कि जिनेवा सम्मेलन का शीघ्र ही पुनः आयोजन किया जाए और उसमें पी एल ओ को प्रतिनिधित्व दिया जाए।

अध्यक्ष महोदय, भारत सब देशों से मैत्री चाहता है और किसी पर प्रभुत्व स्थापित नहीं करना चाहता। भारत न तो आणविक शस्त्र शक्ति है और न बनना ही चाहता है। नयी सरकार ने अपने असंदिग्ध शब्दों में इस बात की पुनर्घोषणा की है। हमारी कार्यसूची का एक सर्वस्पर्षी विषय जो आगामी अनेक वर्षों और दशकों में बना रहेगा वह है मानव का भविष्य। मैं भारत की ओर से इस महासभा को आश्वासन देना चाहता हूँ कि हम एक विश्व के आदर्शों की प्राप्ति और मानव के कल्याण तथा उसके गौरव के लिए त्याग और बलिदान की बेला में कभी पीछे नहीं रहेंगे।

अपनी 13 दिन पुरानी सरकार के गिरने पर श्री अटल बिहारी वाजपेयी द्वारा इस्तीफा देने से पहले का भाषण (1996)

कहा जाता है कि हम केवल काऊ बेल्ट में जीते हैं। किस तरह की आप बात कर रहे हैं। हरियाणा में जीते हैं हमने कर्नाटक में समर्थन प्राप्त किया है। ये ठीक है केरल और तमिलनाडु में हम उतने शक्तिशाली नहीं हैं, मगर हमारा संगठन है। पश्चिम बंगाल में भी हमें 10% से थोड़ा कम वोट मिला हुआ है। इस सदन में एक-एक व्यक्ति की पार्टी है। और वे हमारे खिलाफ जमघट करके हमें हटाने का प्रयास कर रहे हैं। उन्हें प्रयास करने का पूरा अधिकार है। मगर हैं वे एक व्यक्ति की पार्टी, एकला चलो रे। और चलो एकला अपने चुनाव क्षेत्र से। मगर दिल्ली में आकर हो जाओ इकट्ठे रे। किसलिए इकट्ठे हो जाओ, देश के भले के लिए? स्वागत है! हम भी अपने ढंग से देश की सेवा कर रहे हैं। और अगर हम देशभक्त न होते, और अगर हम निस्वार्थ भाव से राजनीति में अपना स्थान बनाने का प्रयास न करते। और हमारे इन प्रयासों के पीछे 40 साल की साधना है।

ये कोई आकस्मिक जनादेश नहीं है, ये कोई चमत्कार नहीं हुआ है। हमने मेहनत की है। हम लोगों में गये हैं। हमने संघर्ष किया है। पार्टी 365 दिन चलने वाली पार्टी है। यह कोई चुनाव में कुकुरमुत्ते की तरह उग आने वाली पार्टी नहीं है। और आज हमें अकारण कटघरे में खड़ा किया जा रहा है। क्योंकि हम थोड़ी ज्यादा सीटें नहीं ला सके। हम मानते हैं कि हमारी कमजोरी है। हमें बहुमत मिलना चाहिए था।

राष्ट्रपति ने हमें अवसर दिया, हमें सफलता नहीं मिली वह अलग बात है। लेकिन फिर भी हम सदन में सबसे बड़े विरोधी दल के रूप में बैठेंगे। और आपको हमारा सहयोग लेकर सदन चलाना पड़ेगा इस बात को मत भूलिये। सदन चलाने

में हम आपको पूरा सहयोग देंगे। ये आश्वासन हम आपको देना चाहते हैं। मगर सरकार आप कैसी बनाएंगे, वो सरकार किस कार्यक्रम पर बनेगी। वो सरकार कैसी चलेगी, मैं नहीं जानता।

जहाँ तक दलितों का सवाल है। शिड्यूल कास्ट के कुल मेंबर हैं 77 और उनमें से 29 मेंबर बीजेपी के चुने गए हैं। सीपीआईएम के 5 मेंबर हैं। सीपीआई का 1 मेंबर है। कांग्रेस के 15 मेंबर हैं। जनता दल के 7 मेंबर हैं। और सबसे ज्यादा हमारे मेंबर हैं। ST यानि शिड्यूल ट्राइब में भी कुल लोग 41 हैं जिनमें बीजेपी के 11 सांसद हैं। हमारा जनाधार नहीं है। हमें लोगों का व्यापक समर्थन प्राप्त नहीं है।

अगर आप हमें छोड़कर सत्ता में रहना चाहते हैं। और सोचते हैं कि वह सरकार टिकाऊ होगी तो मुझे तो उसके टिकने के लक्षण नहीं दिखाई दे रहे हैं। पहले तो उसका जन्म लेना कठिन है, जन्म लेने के बाद जीवित रहना कठिन है। और यह सरकार अंतर्विरोधों में घिरी हुई देश का कितना लाभ कर सकेगी, यह प्रश्नवाचक चिन्ह है। हर बात के लिए आपको कांग्रेस के पास दौड़ना पड़ेगा। और जब आप उन पर निर्भर हो जायेंगे। अभी तो मैं नहीं जानता। पहले चर्चा हुई थी कि कुछ शर्तें लगाई जा रही हैं। फिर पता चला कि कॉर्डिनेशन कमेटी बनाई जायेगी। सदन में भी हम कार्डिनेशन करते हैं। आप बिना कॉर्डिनेशन के देश चलाना चाहते हैं।

हम संख्या बल के आगे सिर झुकाते हैं और आपको विश्वास दिलाते हैं कि जो काम हमने अपने हाथ में लिया है। उसे जब तक पूरा नहीं कर लेते तब तक आराम से नहीं बैठेंगे।

अध्यक्ष महोदय, मैं अपना त्यागपत्र राष्ट्रपति महोदय को देने जा रहा हूँ।

15 अगस्त 2003 को तत्कालीन प्रधान मंत्री अटल बिहारी वाजपेयी द्वारा लाल किले की प्राचीर से दिये अंतिम भाषण के मुख्य अंश

पिछले साल देश में सूखा रहा, हमने सभी सूखाग्रस्त इलाकों को पर्याप्त मदद दी और पर्याप्त अन्न भेजा। किसानों को बधाई जिन्होंने अपनी कड़ी मेहनत से देश के अन्न के भंडार भर दिये। आज भारत की अर्थव्यवस्था विश्व की चौथी बड़ी

अर्थव्यवस्था बन गई है। सभी, वैज्ञानिकों, शिक्षकों, साहित्यकारों और कलाकारों तथा बच्चों को इसके लिए बधाई।

सभी प्रवासी भारतीयों का अभिनंदन, विश्व में भारत की प्रतिष्ठा बढ़ाने में उनका उल्लेखनीय योगदान है, हमें उन पर गर्व है। स्वतंत्रता के संघर्ष में जिस महान भारत का सपना हमने देखा था, कुछ साकार हुआ है और कुछ होना बाक़ी है।

राष्ट्र की सुरक्षा हमारे लिए सर्वोपरि है। इसलिए 5 साल पहले हमारी सरकार ने जो पहला काम किया वह अणु परीक्षण था। भारत को आर्थिक और सामाजिक दृष्टि से अधिक शक्तिशाली बनाने की जरूरत है।

5 सालों में हमारी विदेश नीति ने विश्व में भारत की प्रतिष्ठा बढ़ाई है। पाकिस्तान के साथ रिश्तों में हाल के दिनों में कुछ प्रगति हुई है लेकिन आतंकी गतिविधियां अब भी जारी हैं। पाकिस्तान के मित्रों से मैं कहता रहा हूं कि लड़ते-लड़ते 50 साल हो गए हैं, और कितना खून बहाना बाकी है? लाहौर से आई 2 साल की बच्ची नूर को हिंदुस्तान में जो प्यार मिला उसमें ऐसा पैगाम है जिसे पाकिस्तान को समझना जरूरी है। दोनों देशों के स्वाधीनता दिवस के मौके पर मैं पाकिस्तान को अमन के रास्ते पर साथ चलने का न्यौता देता हूं।

स्वतंत्र चुनाव ने एक बार फिर साबित कर दिया है कि कश्मीर की जनता ने सीमा पार आतंक को ठुकरा दिया है। जम्मू-कश्मीर की गुत्थी को बातचीत के जरिए ही सुलझाया जा सकता है।

पिछले कुछ सालों में देश ने जो प्रगति की है उसने मुझे नई आशा और विश्वास दिया है, कर्ज लेने वाला भारत आज कर्ज दे रहा है, हमेशा विदेशी मुद्रा की कमी झेलने वाले भारत ने आज 100 अरब डालर विदेशी मुद्रा कमा ली है। जरूरत की चीजों की कीमतें काबू में हैं और बाजार में किसी चीज का अभाव नहीं है, गरीबी घट रही है, और तेजी से घटाने का हमारा संकल्प है।

आजादी के 50 साल बाद भी लगभग 2 लाख गांव ऐसे थे जिनमें सड़कें नहीं पहुंची थीं, हमारी सरकार ने पहली बार इन गावों को अच्छी सड़कों से जोड़ने के लिए प्रधानमंत्री ग्राम सड़क योजना शुरू की है। आजादी के 50 सालों में सिर्फ 550 किलोमीटर के 4 लेन वाले राजमार्ग बनाए गए थे, अब हम रोजाना 11 किलोमीटर की गति से 24,000 किलोमीटर सड़कें बनाएंगे। 54,000 किलोमीटर की राष्ट्रीय राजमार्ग योजना पर काम शुरू हो गया है।

कंप्यूटर के क्षेत्र में लाखों नौजवानों को रोजगार मिला है। सॉफ्टवेयर का निर्यात 8,000 करोड़ रुपए से बढ़कर अब 50,000 करोड़ रुपए हो गया है।

भारत चंद्रमा पर अपना अंतरिक्ष यान भेजेगा, इसका नाम होगा चंद्रयान प्रथम।

पिछले दशकों में हरित क्रांति और श्वेत क्रांति के जरिए भारत की कृषि को काफी बल मिला है। अब भारत के लिए जरूरी है खाद्य शृंखला क्रांति, जिसका लक्ष्य वर्ष 2010 तक भारत के किसान की औसत आमदनी को दोगुना करना है।

अंत्योदय अन्न योजना के अंतर्गत देश के अत्यंत गरीब डेढ़ करोड़ परिवारों के लिए 2 रुपए किलो गेहूं और 3 रुपए किलो चावल के अंतर्गत हर महीने 2 रुपए किलो गेहूं और 3 रुपए किलो चावल, हर महीने 35 किलो अनाज दिए जाने का काम हो रहा है, इतना सस्ता अनाज कभी नहीं दिया गया। यह दुनिया की सबसे बड़ी खाद्य सुरक्षा योजना है।

सर्व शिक्षा अभियान के चलते अब कोई भी बालक, विषेशकर बालिकाएं अब प्राइमरी शिक्षा से वंचित नहीं रहेंगे। 2.5 लाख शिक्षकों की नियुक्ति इसी साल की जाएगी। प्राइमरी तक के बच्चों को दोपहर का भोजन देने का कार्यक्रम कुछ राज्यों में चल रहा है, अब इसे पूरे देश में चलाने का फैसला किया है। बाद में 10वीं तक के छात्रों के लिए भी इसे लागू किया जाएगा। यह राष्ट्रीय कार्यक्रम अक्षय पात्र के नाम से चलेगा।

देश के पिछड़े राज्यों में अच्छे अस्पतालों की कमी से होने वाली परेशानियों को मै जानता हूं, इसलिए दिल्ली के एम्स जैसी सुविधाओं वाले 6 अस्पताल देश के पिछड़े राज्यों में अगले 3 सालों के दौरान खोले जाएंगे।

पिछले 5 साल में जिस गति से गांवों और शहरों में मकानों का निर्माण हुआ है वह पहले कभी नहीं हुआ था। अब जितनी कम ब्याज दर पर मकानों के लिए कर्ज मिल रहा है वह पहले कभी नहीं मिल रहा था।

भारत एक बहुधर्मी देश है और मजहब के आधार पर भेदभाव करना हमारी प्रकृति और संस्कृति के खिलाफ है। अल्पसंख्यकों की हिफाजत और उनकी भलाई के प्रति हमें हमेशा जागरूक रहना है।

उत्तर पूर्व के राज्यों में शांति वार्ता के अच्छे नतीजे निकल रहे हैं। बंदूक उठाने वाले हाथ अब वहां के विकास में लगना चाहते हैं। सरकार उनके स्वागत के लिए तैयार है।

हम सबका दायित्व है कि अपनी अनुसूचित जातियों और जनजातियों तथा पिछड़े वर्गों के बंधुओं को समान अवसर उपलब्ध कराकर व्यवस्था में भागीदार

बनाएं। आदिवासियों के विकास के लिए हमने नया मंत्रालय और आयोग बनाया है। 50 साल के बाद पहली बार अनुसूचित जनजाति की सूची की समीक्षा करके 100 से भी अधिक नए समूहों को इसमें जोड़ा गया है।

महिलाओं के सशक्तिकरण के लिए संसद और विधानसभाओं में 33% आरक्षण दिए जाने का प्रस्ताव है। आज पंचायतों और नगर पालिकाओं में 10 लाख से भी ज्यादा महिला सदस्य हैं।

प्यारे देशवासियो आज देश ऐसे मोड़ पर है जहां से देश एक लंबी छलांग लगा सकता है। 2020 तक भारत को विकसित राष्ट्र बनाने के बड़े ध्येय को हासिल करने की तमन्ना सारे देश में बल पकड़ रही है। जरा पीछे मुड़कर देखिए, बड़े बड़े संकटों का सामना करके भारत आगे बढ़ रहा है।

PRIME MINISTER VAJPAYEE'S ADDRESS TO THE JOINT SESSION OF THE UNITED STATES CONGRESS ON SEPTEMBER 14, 2000

The House adopted a resolution congratulating India and my government on the successful elections completed in October 1999. This display of broad-based bipartisan support for strengthening relations with India is heartening.

It is a source of encouragement to both President Clinton and to me, as we work together to infuse a new quality in our ties. I thank you for the nearunique approach that you have adopted towards my country.

Those of you who saw the warm response to President Clinton's speech to our Parliament in March this year will recognise that similar cross-party support exists in India as well for deeper engagement with the USA.

I am also deeply touched by the resolution adopted in the House two days ago welcoming my visit and the prospect of closer Indo-US understanding.

Mr Speaker,

American people have shown that democracy and individual liberty provide the conditions in which knowledge progresses, science discovers, innovation occurs, enterprise thrives and, ultimately, people advance.

To more than a million and half from my country, America is now home. In turn, their industry, enterprise and skills are contributing to the advancement of American society.

I see in the outstanding success of the Indian community in America, a metaphor of the vast potential that exists in Indo-US relations, and what we can achieve together.

Just as American experience has been a lesson in what people can achieve in a democratic framework, India has been the laboratory of a democratic process rising to meet the strongest challenges that can be flung at it.

In the half century of our independent existence, we have woven an exquisite tapestry. Out of diversity we have brought unity. The several languages of India speak with one voice under the roof of our Parliament.

In your remarkable experiment as a nation state, you have proven the same truth. Out of the huddled masses that you welcomed to your shores you have created a great nation.

For me the most gratifying of the many achievements of Indian democracy has been the change it has brought to the lives of the weak and the vulnerable.

To give just one figure, in recent years it has enabled more than a million women in small towns and distant villages to enter local elected councils and to decide on issues that touch upon their lives.

Two years ago, while much of Asia was convulsed by economic crisis, India held its course.

In the last ten years, we have grown at 6.5% per year: that puts India among the ten fastest growing economies of the world.

Economic activity gets more and more diversified by the year: President Clinton and many among the friends gathered here have had occasion to glimpse our advances in information technology.

We are determined to sustain the momentum of our economy: our aim is to double our per capita income in ten years — and that means we must grow at 9% a year.

To achieve this order of growth we have ushered in comprehensive reforms. We are committed to releasing the creative genius of our people, the entrepreneurial skills of the men and women of the country, of its scientists and craftsmen. At the same time, we in India, remain committed to the primacy of the State in fulfilling its social obligations to the deprived, the weak and the poor.

Important sectors of the country's infrastructure - power, insurance, banking, telecom - are being opened to private initiative, domestic and foreign.

Trade barriers are being lowered.

Mr Speaker, ladies and gentlemen,

There are forces outside our country that believe that they can use terror to unravel the territorial integrity of India. They wish to show that a multireligious society cannot exist.

They pursue a task in which they are doomed to fail.

No country has faced as ferocious an attack of terrorist violence as India has over the past two decades: 21,000 were killed by foreign sponsored terrorists in Punjab alone, 16,000 have been killed in Jammu and Kashmir.

As many of you here in the Congress have in recent hearings recognised a stark fact: no region is a greater source of terrorism than our neighbourhood.

Indeed, in our neighbourhood - in this, the 21st century - religious war has not just been fashioned into, it has been proclaimed to be, an instrument of State policy.

Distance offers no insulation. It should not cause complacence.

You know, and I know: such evil cannot succeed.

But even in foiling it could inflict untold suffering.

That is why the United States and India have begun to deepen their cooperation for combating terrorism. We must redouble these efforts.

Mr. Speaker, ladies and gentlemen,

There was a time when we were on the other side of each other's globes. Today, on the digital map, India and the United States are neighbours and partners.

India and the United States have taken the lead in shaping the information age. Over the last decade, this new technology has sustained American prosperity in a way that has challenged conventional wisdom on economic growth.

We are two nations blessed with extraordinary resources and talent. Measured in terms of the industries of tomorrow, we are together defining the partnerships of the future.

But our two countries have the potential to do more to shape the character of the global economy in this century.

We should turn the example of our own cooperation into a partnership that uses the possibilities of the new technologies for defining new ways of fighting poverty, illiteracy, hunger, disease and pollution.

Mr Speaker, ladies and gentlemen,

We believe that India and America can – and should – march hand in hand towards a world in which economic conditions improve for all.

A situation that provides comfortable living standards to one-third of the world's population, but condemns the remaining two-thirds to poverty and want, is unsustainable.

The foremost responsibility that the 21st century has cast on all of us is to change this unacceptable legacy of the past.

It should be our common endeavour to overcome this legacy. I, therefore, propose a comprehensive global dialogue on development.

We would be happy to offer New Delhi as the venue for this dialogue.

In this Congress, you have often expressed concern about the future contours of Asia. Will it be an Asia that will be at peace with itself? Or will it be a continent, where countries seek to redraw boundaries and settle claims – historical or imaginary – through force?

We seek an Asia where power does not threaten stability and security. We do not want the domination of some to crowd out the space for others. We must create an Asia where cooperative rather than aggressive assertion of national self-interests defines behaviour among nations.

If we want an Asia fashioned on such ideals – a democratic, prosperous, tolerant, pluralistic, stable Asia – if we want an Asia where our vital interests are secure, then it is necessary for us to re-examine old assumptions.

It is imperative for India and the United States to work together more closely in pursuit of those goals. In the years ahead, a strong, democratic and economically prosperous India, standing at the crossroads of all the major cultural and economic zones of Asia, will be an indispensable factor of stability in the region.

Our cooperation for peace and stability requires us to also define the principles of our own engagement. We must be prepared to accommodate our respective concerns.

We must have the mutual confidence to acknowledge our respective roles and complementary responsibilities in areas of vital importance to each of us.

Security issues have cast a shadow on our relationship. I believe this is unnecessary. We have much in common and no clash of interests.

We both share a commitment to ultimately eliminating nuclear weapons. We have both declared voluntary moratoriums on testing.

India understands your concerns. We do not wish to unravel your non-proliferation efforts. We wish you to understand our security concerns.

We are at a historic moment in our ties. As we embark on our common endeavour to build a new relationship, we must give practical shape to our shared belief that democracies can be friends, partners and allies.

In recent years, through all the good and difficult times, we have spoken to each other more often than we have ever done in the past. I thank President Clinton for this leadership and vision in steering this dialogue. I sincerely thank members of this Congress for supporting and encouraging this process.

As we talk with candour, we open the doors to new possibilities and new areas of cooperation – in advancing democracy, in combating terrorism, in energy and environment, science and technology and in international peacekeeping. And, we are discovering that our shared values and common interests are leading us to seek a natural partnership of shared endeavours.

India and the United States have taken a decisive step away from the past. The dawn of the new century has marked a new beginning in our relations.

Let us work to fulfill the promise and the hope of today.

Let us remove the shadow of hesitation that lies between us and our joint vision.

Let us use the strength of all that we have in common to build together a future that we wish for ourselves and for the world that we live in.

Thank you.

1

Sarva Shiksha Abhiyan

1. INTRODUCTION

Sarva Shiksha Abhiyan (Education for All Movement), is a government programme aimed at the universalisation of elementary education "in a time bound manner", as mandated by the 86th Amendment to the Constitution of India making free and compulsory education to children between the ages of 6 to 14 (estimated to be 205 million children in 2001) a fundamental right. The programme was pioneered by the then Prime Minister Atal Bihari Vajpayee.

As an intervention programme, it started in 2002 though Sarva Shiksha Abhiyan has been operational since 2000-2001. However, its roots go back to 1993-1994, when the District Primary Education Programme (DPEP) was launched, with an aim of achieving the objective of universal primary education. DPEP, over several phases, covered 272 districts in 18 states of the country. The expenditure on the programme was shared by the Central Government (85%) and the State Governments. The Central share was funded by a number of external agencies, including the World Bank, Department for International Development (DFID) and UNICEF. By 2001, more than $ 1,500 million had been committed to the programme, and 50 million children covered in its ambit. In an impact assessment of Phase I of DPEP, the planners concluded that its net impact on minority children was impressive, while there was little evidence of any impact on the enrolment of girls. Nevertheless, they concluded that the investment in DPEP was not a waste, because it introduced a new approach to primary school interventions in India.

The Right to Education Act (RTE) came into force on 1 April 2010. Some educationists and policy makers believe that, with the passing of this act, Sarva Shiksha Abhiyan has acquired the necessary legal force for its implementation.

Sarva Shiksha Abhiyan (SSA) programme aimed at Universal Elementary Education was launched in January 2001 to provide useful and relevant education for all children in the age group of 6-14 years by 2010. It is an attempt to provide an opportunity for improving human capabilities to all children, with special focus on bridging social, regional and gender gaps, through the active participation of the community in the management of schools.

1.1 Objectives of Sarva Shiksha Abhiyan

- All children in School, Education Guarantee Centre, Alternate School, 'Back-to-School' camp by 2003; extended to 2005.
- Bridge all gender and social category gaps at primary stage by 2007, and at elementary education level by 2010.
- Universal retention by 2010.
- Focus on elementary education of satisfactory quality with emphasis on education for life.

1.2 The objectives are expressed nationally though it is expected that various districts and states would achieve universalisation in their own respective contexts and in their own time frame. 2010 is the outer limit for such achievements. The emphasis is on mainstreaming out-of-school children through diverse strategies and on providing eight years of schooling for all children in 6-14 age groups. Within this framework it is expected that the education system will be made relevant so that children and parents find the schooling system useful and absorbing according to their natural and social environment.

1.3 The programme covers the entire country and all schools except private unaided schools. Under the scheme, regular schools/alternative schooling facilities are to be provided within one km of every habitation, strengthen existing school infrastructure through provision of additional classrooms, toilets, drinking water, to improve teacher strength through recruitment of additional teachers, capacity building of teachers by extensive training, provision of grant for developing teacher-learning material and development of academic support infrastructure.

Features of Interventions

1.4 Sarva Shiksha Abhiyan is moulded within a fixed framework from planning and implementation of specific interventions and actions to financial provisions for elementary education.

Major Interventions

1. Provision for opening of new schools or for setting up EGS (Education Guarantee Scheme) centres in unserved habitations.
2. Opening of Upper primary schools.
3. Interventions to mainstream out of school children, dropouts.
4. Inclusive education and other activities.
5. Block resource/cluster resource centres.
6. Innovative activity for girls' education, early childhood care and education.

7. Capacity building for teachers, training, teacher grant, recruitment of teachers
8. Civil works, additional classrooms, maintenance grant, school grant.
9. Management cost, research and evaluation, community training.

Limitations of the Study

1.5 Some limitations were encountered that may have impacted the findings of the study.

1. Inadequate quantitative information on enrolment of dropouts and out of school children to assess the effectiveness of strategies to mainstream these children.
2. Sample size variations across states
   (a) Evaluation teams in villages with high density of schools canvassed more schools than in those which were underserved.
   (b) One additional town (Secunderabad) was canvassed in Andhra Pradesh but dwellings in the slums in this town were not canvassed.
   (c) Upper primary students in slum schools in West Bengal and Uttar Pradesh were not canvassed.
3. Weak linkages between urban local bodies and nodal agencies resulting in poor availability of data for urban slum samples.

2. OBJECTIVES AND METHODOLOGY

The Development Advisory Evaluation Committee under the chairmanship of the Deputy Chairman, Planning Commission had directed the PEO to conduct an evaluation on the performance of the SSA scheme. The study was designed in consultation with MHRD and the field survey was conducted over a period of four months beginning from February 2008. In some states the survey was completed in June 2008 as schools had closed for summer vacations.

2.1 The broad objectives for the study:

1. To assess the extent to which SSA has been able to achieve its objectives and related targets and the factors determining the same.
2. To assess the extent to which the approach/strategies adopted under SSA to achieve the objectives were effective.
3. To identify constraints in the implementation of the scheme.
4. To suggest the way forward.

Keeping in view the broad objectives of "Sarva Shiksha Abhiyan", the specific objectives of this Evaluation Study were grouped in three categories:

2.2 Access

1. To assess the extent of attendance and enrolment of children in the relevant age group and to analyse the reasons thereof.
2. To assess the extent to which unserved and underserved villages/habitations have been provided access to schooling through formal schools.
3. To study the strategies adopted for bringing the dropout and out of school children into school and retaining them.

2.3 Equity

1. To assess the equity maintained through the programme with respect to social groups, gender and children with special needs.

2.4 Quality

1. To assess quality indicators such as PTR, achievement level of children, attendance of teachers etc.

2. To examine the availability and adequacy of the infrastructural facilities in the schools.
3. To assess the level and nature of partnership between central, state and local self government and to examine their role in school management.
4. To assess the financial aspects of SSA in terms of centre-state contributions, timeliness of transfer of funds, utilization etc and the role of development partners.
5. To identify constraints in the implementation of the scheme and suggest remedial measures.

Methodology

2.5 Sampling Method

A multistage stratified sampling was adopted for selection of samples at State and district levels.

Criteria for selection of samples

2.6 Selection of States

The States were classified on the basis of location in five zones ie, North, West, East, South and North East. States in each zone were stratified on the basis of percentage expenditure incurred in the 10th Five Year Plan. Data on rural samples were collected through sample surveys conducted in ten states and one UT and data for urban samples from twelve towns in five states and one UT. However all the states and UTs (35) were requested to fill in the State level/UT level schedules.

2.7 Selection of Districts

Districts were selected on the basis of female literacy and availability of DISE data for the year 2002-2003. The criteria used for the selection of the number of districts was based on the total number of districts in the selected states.

2.8 Selection of Blocks/Villages

From each district, two blocks were selected randomly while ensuring that they were not adjacent to each other.

From each selected block the list of all revenue villages in that block and number with types of schools (only primary and upper-primary and funded under SSA) in those villages were obtained. From this list two villages were selected using following criteria:

(i) One village having more than two schools and with at least one upper primary school under SSA, and

(ii) One village having only one primary school under SSA.

2.9 Selection of Schools/Students

In each selected village all the existing schools belonging to different category of schools covered under SSA ie government, government-aided and Local bodies/EGS/ A&IE centre were selected. From each school, eight students were randomly selected (four from Class II and four from class VI) and answers to a set of questions in English, Local language and Mathematics were solicited to assess their learning achievement levels.

2.10 Selection of Households

In each village ten households having children in the age group of 6-14 years were selected through snowball sampling.

2.11 Sample Size and Selection of Urban Samples

For selection of urban samples, from each zone one state with highest slum population was selected and two towns were selected from that state. Two towns from Puducherry (UT) were also selected. Two slums were selected from each selected town.

2.12 Selection of Focus Groups

From each sample village one Focus Group Discussion was organized consisting of parents (8-10 persons) each belonging to

(a) SC and/or ST (depending upon their availability and concentration).

(b) Non-SC/ST.

(c) parents of out of school children and dropouts and other knowledgeable persons of the village.

2.13 Instruments

Structured questionnaires were prepared at various levels to generate primary and secondary information. The following instruments were used for collection of quantitative and qualitative information.

1. State Level Schedule (SLS)
2. District Level Schedule (DLS)
3. Block Level Schedule (BLS)/Town Level Schedule (TLS)
4. Village Level Schedule (VLS)/Slum Level Schedule (SmLS)
5. School Level Schedule (ScLS)
6. Student Level Schedule (CLS)
7. Observation based check list at school level (OBCL)
8. Household/Dwelling Level Schedule (HLS/DwLS)
9. Focus Group Discussions at Village level.

2.14 Reference Period

The reference period of the study was from 2003 to 2007.

3. UNIVERSAL ACCESS AND EQUITY

3.1 In recognition of the right of every child to access schooling facilities within his/her neighbourhood one of the key interventions of SSA to provide universal access is to extend coverage to unserved and underserved locations by providing a primary school within 1 km of the habitation and an upper primary school within 3 kms of the habitation.

Unserved Habitations

3.2 The Seventh All India Educational Survey (2002) identified 1,47,928 habitations (13% of total habitations at that time) with no primary schools within 1 km or any alternative schools. In 2007, the number of unserved habitations had declined considerably across all states though Andhra Pradesh (2,234), Bihar (2,903), Chhattisgarh (3,741), Rajasthan (3,121) and Uttar Pradesh (9,897) had a large number of habitations without access to primary schools or Education Guarantee Schemes (EGS) centres.

3.3 Most states used a two pronged strategy by opening new primary schools and setting up EGS centres in unserved habitations. New primary schools were opened in Andhra Pradesh, Bihar, Haryana, Madhya Pradesh, Rajasthan, Tamil Nadu and Uttar Pradesh. No new schools were opened in Assam, Himachal Pradesh and West Bengal as these states either reported that adequate number of schools were within accessible distance or that the state norms for schooling facilities were different (Himachal Pradesh - 1.5 km).

3.4 EGS centres/Alternative and Innovative Education centres (AIE) were opened in all states to mainstream out of school children and in small habitations that did not qualify for a regular school. Even in these cases distance, population norms (separately for tribal and non-tribal areas) and/or enrolment norms (minimum of 15/10 children) were followed. Except in Assam, Chandigarh and West Bengal, in other states EGS centres which were functioning for more than two years were upgraded into regular schools. Some EGS centres in Andhra Pradesh were closed down due to non-functioning centres and in Himachal Pradesh due to insufficient enrolment. Assam, Chandigarh, Madhya Pradesh, Uttar Pradesh and West Bengal continued to have a large number of EGS/AIE centres.

3.5 There were intra-district variations in the provision of access to schools. In Chittoor district of Andhra Pradesh, Madanpalle block had schooling facilities in all villages whereas in Pakal block there were 161 habitations without any schooling facilities. Similarly in Binnabari Gram Panchayat of Khoribari block, Siliguri district (West Bengal) 90 habitations (in tea gardens, forest areas) were without any schooling facilities. Formation of new habitations over time, non-availability of land for construction, poor community involvement, procedural delays (sanction not received for opening primary schools), lack of skill at the village level for undertaking construction of civil works, inadequate funds (cost norms) has impeded universal access.

3.6 At the village level, the most number of new primary schools (opened within the preceding five years) could be surveyed in Haryana, Madhya Pradesh and Uttar Pradesh. In Assam and West Bengal all sampled schools were more than 20 years old. In Rajasthan, 47% of the schools were less than 10 years but more than 5 years old. Though a large number of EGS centres have been opened in Assam, no EGS centre were found in the selected villages. AIE centres were functioning in Chandigarh, Haryana, Himachal Pradesh, Tamil Nadu and West Bengal. In terms of new investments in infrastructure, Bihar, Madhya Pradesh, Rajasthan, Tamil Nadu and Uttar Pradesh did considerably better than Andhra Pradesh, Assam, Himachal Pradesh and West Bengal.

Underserved Habitations

3.7 The SSA norm stipulates that as per requirement based on the number of children completing primary education, up to a ceiling of one upper primary school/section for every two primary school/sections may be opened. It was observed that the classification of primary schools is not uniform as some states classify primary as classes I-IV and some states consider class V to be a part of the primary school. Further, while states such as Assam and Madhya Pradesh had a large number of single primary and upper primary schools, in Bihar, Rajasthan and Tamil Nadu, there were composite schools as well (primary integrated with upper primary). Some secondary schools too had upper primary sections. Thus no definitive conclusions could be reached on the ratio of upper primary to primary schools in the selected samples. However, the ratio of upper primary to primary schools in most states was unfavourable (as per the state report cards).

3.8 In terms of accessibility to upper primary schools in the neighbourhood of habitations, it was observed that 50% of villages in Bihar, Haryana, Himachal Pradesh, Madhya Pradesh and Rajasthan had only single primary schools and no upper primary schools. Even though a number of primary schools were reported to have been upgraded into upper primary schools in the selected blocks in Bihar and Madhya Pradesh, the fact that there are a large number of underserved villages indicates the need for providing access to upper primary schools/sections in close proximity to habitations to reduce absenteeism and dropouts.

Distance from Schools

3.9 To ascertain accessibility in terms of the distance of the school from the habitation, the students' responses to 'how far is your school from your house' were analysed.

3.10 More than 98% of the habitations had access to elementary schools within 3 kms of their habitations and 88% of the students were attending elementary schools located within 1 km of their homes. In Andhra Pradesh, Assam, Haryana, Himachal Pradesh, Madhya Pradesh, Tamil Nadu and West Bengal a few children in the selected villages travel more than 3 kms to their schools which is consistent with the observation that the villages had few upper primary schools. In Haryana, one AIE centre set up recently for primary students was located more than one km away from the village. Transportation facilities need to be provided for children living in remote habitations as has been done in Andhra Pradesh. In Haryana and Madhya

Pradesh, bicycles are provided to girls enrolled in upper primary sections outside the village.

PRI Participation

3.11 The availability of schools by type of management indicates that the majority of the schools in the villages are government schools (including government-aided and local body schools). In the selected villages more than 90% of the schools were government schools. At the block level, 75% of the schools were government schools. The participation of local governing bodies (Panchayati Raj Institutions) in school management which is perceived to provide a better interface with the community and improve decentralized planning and implementation was predominant in the southern states of Andhra Pradesh and Tamil Nadu and to some extent in Rajasthan. In Assam, Bihar, Uttar Pradesh and West Bengal there were few local body schools in the selected blocks implying that these schools are not widely prevalent and may be available in some pockets/villages. In Rajasthan, the PRI participation was better in the non-selected villages in the block. Interestingly, in the villages in Haryana and Rajasthan private schools have a visible presence.

Enrolment and Attendance

3.12 The enrolment rates increased sharply as a result of the efforts to provide more primary schools, upper primary schools, EGS centres in unserved habitations and AIE centres for out of school children. Other interventions such as enrolment drives, improvement in infrastructure in schools, incentives such as free books, free uniforms, midday meals also contributed to the improvement in enrolment ratios from 89.5% in 2003 to 92.9% in 2007 in the selected samples.

3.13 Across states, the enrolment rates increased rapidly in Assam, Bihar, Chandigarh, Madhya Pradesh, Rajasthan and

Uttar Pradesh, remained stagnant in Andhra Pradesh, Tamil Nadu and declined in Haryana, Himachal Pradesh and West Bengal.

3.14 Enrolment declined in five of the selected blocks as a result of the decline in child population of 6-14 years and/or possibly due to outward migration. Guhala and Mahendragarh (Haryana) reported a decline of 35.8% and 10.7% in child population in 2007 as compared to 2003. Bharmour, Bijhari and Nadaun (Himachal Pradesh) reported decline in child population of 6.2%, 7.8% and 1.3% respectively in 2007. In nine blocks, child population was reported to have declined but enrolment increased and in three blocks though child population declined there was no impact on enrolment.

3.15 Enrolment declined in six other blocks but was not caused by decline in child population. In Khairabad (Rajasthan), Palacode (Tamil Nadu), Baheri and Malasa (Uttar Pradesh), Matigara and Haringhata-I (West Bengal) though child population registered an increase, enrolment ratios declined either due to shift to private schools, decline in overaged children enrolled in the schools or children dropping out due to lack of upper primary schools. In West Bengal, the decline in enrolment in Khoribari block was recorded due to administrative reasons ie., the division of the block into two circles.

3.16 Improved access to schools had a positive impact on school attendance as 62% of the schools reported student attendance of more than 75%. However, student absenteeism was high in Assam, Bihar and Uttar Pradesh. In Chandigarh, poor attendance was reported from AIE centres.

3.17 Students reported distance from school, work at home (sibling care), helping parents, ill health, festival and seasonal migration as some of the reasons for irregular attendance. Though 85% of the students mentioned they would continue coming to school even if midday meals were stopped and 86% of the parents reported that they would continue to send their children to schools even if midday meal were withdrawn, 40% of the schools in Assam and Bihar did not provide midday meals. AIE centres in Narnaul (Haryana) and in few centres in West Bengal also did not provide CMDM. In a research study by IIT Guwahati, lack of adequate recreational facilities in schools in Assam and poor parental motivation were identified as causal factors for absenteeism. In Assam, Bihar and Uttar Pradesh, improved enrolment rates were not reflected in better attendance rates.

Out of School Children

3.18 Notwithstanding the improvement in enrolment ratios, villages in Bihar and Uttar Pradesh had a large number of out of school children.

3.19 7.2% of the sampled households had dropouts or out of school children (OOSC) and more than half of these children belong to socially disadvantaged groups (SC/ST). In Haryana, Himachal Pradesh and Madhya Pradesh all the out of school children were from SC/ST households. Dropouts accounted for 76.6% of the children remaining out of school.

3.20 Gender disparity exists as 55% of the dropouts/OOSCs were girls. A majority of the out of school children in Rajasthan were girls. Among the major reasons for being out of school were "work at home" in Bihar, Himachal Pradesh, West Bengal and sibling care in Rajasthan and Uttar Pradesh. In Haryana and Uttar Pradesh a larger share of dropouts were boys for reasons reported as "outside work". In a household survey conducted by state government of Tamil Nadu in 2005, migration, earning compulsion, household work and failure were reported to be causes for children remaining out of schools.

3.21 70% of the out of school children were willing to attend schools and their expectations from school, teachers and parents were free uniforms, good infrastructure in schools, scholarship, good quality teaching (Uttar Pradesh, West Bengal), no punishment (Bihar, Rajasthan), teachers being punctual (Himachal Pradesh, Uttar Pradesh) and parents to refrain from giving work at home (Bihar, West Bengal).

3.22 Enrolment drives combined with awareness generation need to be undertaken on a more regular and systematic basis as only 38% of the parents could recall that enrolment drives were undertaken in the recent years. Awareness regarding SSA schemes was lacking in 45% of the households. The largest numbers of households which were aware of SSA were in Tamil Nadu (96%), Assam (90.8%) and Bihar (80%). The least aware were in Uttar Pradesh (18%), Rajasthan (33%), Haryana (36%), Himachal Pradesh (41%) and Madhya Pradesh (44%).

3.23 The presence of pre-primary component in schools affects the incidence of out of school children as girls are freed from the burden of looking after siblings. It was observed that in the selected villages in Bihar, Rajasthan and Uttar Pradesh with a large number of dropouts, there were no pre-primary sections attached to primary schools. On the other hand, 75% of the schools in Assam and all the schools in Chandigarh had primary schools with pre-primary sections and no dropouts and out of school children were reported in the selected villages in these states.

3.24 A "no detention" policy for children in the primary sections was adopted only in Chandigarh and West Bengal. Failure rates in 2007 in the primary sections (Class I and II) in schools was high in Assam and Madhya Pradesh and children not appearing in exams was high in Haryana, Rajasthan and Madhya Pradesh. Failure rates may be high on account of poor quality of teaching in single teacher schools (Assam), multi-grade schools (Madhya Pradesh) while seasonal migration as in the case of Haryana and Rajasthan prevents a large number of children from appearing in term end examinations. A child friendly curriculum and liberal assessment mechanisms (instead of several unit tests and examinations) can help to promote a culture of learning. Devising of the academic calendar in sync with migratory seasons in migration prone areas, migratory cards and establishment of seasonal hostels can lead to improvement in retention rates.

3.25 All the states follow the same set of activities as set out in the Central Government framework for mainstreaming out of school children such as setting up EGS/AIE centres, residential or non-residential bridge courses, vocational camps for girls, mobile schools etc. In many states, seasonal schools such as sakhar schools for sugarcane workers in Maharashtra or boat schools, sand schools etc in Andhra Pradesh were opened to cater to the needs of migrant labourers. In Bihar, vidyalay chalo kendras were functional in most schools which appear to have attracted many dropouts and out of school children.

Bridging Gaps

3.26 To bring about an improvement in gender parity ratio and social parity ratio SSA laid a strong focus on equity with all interventions providing for an inclusive approach.

3.27 The education system has been made responsive to the needs of the girls through targeted interventions which serve as a pull factor to enhance access and retention of girls in schools and on the other hand to generate a community demand for girls education through training and mobilisation. This was to be achieved through recruitment of female teachers to achieve a 50% female teacher ratio as they play role models for young girls, separate toilets for girls in schools, incentives such as free textbooks, scholarships and uniforms.

3.28 In addition to the above, the National Programme for Education of Girls at Elementary Level (NPEGEL), a special component of SSA was started in 2003 in 2600 educationally backward blocks with interventions focused on gender sensitization, opening of model schools, provision of escort services, stationary and intensive community mobilisation efforts.

3.29 As a result of these interventions, the overall Gender Parity ratio improved from 0.87 in 2003 to 0.89 in 2007. Except in Andhra Pradesh, Himachal Pradesh and Madhya Pradesh, the enrolment ratios of girls had risen across most states. Gender Parity ratio in Assam, Uttar Pradesh and West Bengal was more than 0.90.

3.30 In the educationally backward blocks, the rate of increase in the girls' enrolment was significant. The enrolment of girls in Jalore (Rajasthan) rose by 25% and in Kasba Nagar block of Bihar, by 14%. The NPEGEL schemes were in operation in all the EBBs in the selected districts except in Andhra Pradesh (137 out of 146 blocks), Bihar (32 out of 35 blocks) and West Bengal (2 out of 5 blocks). In Haryana, bicycles and school bags had been distributed to deserving beneficiaries. Hobby/Vocational and remedial classes were organized at cluster centres in Andhra Pradesh and Himachal Pradesh.

3.31 Schools in Andhra Pradesh, Assam, Bihar, Haryana, Himachal Pradesh, Madhya Pradesh, Rajasthan and West Bengal had lower ratios of female teachers than the SSA norm. All male teacher schools were prevalent in Assam (62%), Bihar (32%), Madhya Pradesh (44%) Rajasthan (47%) and Uttar Pradesh (21.9%). Girls' enrolment in all male teacher schools increased in Assam, Bihar and in Madhya Pradesh and declined in Rajasthan and Uttar Pradesh. This indicates that though there are regional variations, improvement in girls' enrolment cannot be attributed to induction of more female teachers in schools.

3.32 In addition to free textbooks, other incentives such as free uniforms and scholarships of small amounts ie ₹15 per month has been provided to SC/ST girls in primary schools in Madhya Pradesh, scholarships in few schools in Himachal

Pradesh, for all primary level girl children in Uttar Pradesh and attendance incentives to girl students in Maharashtra.

3.33 Innovative state schemes are also in operation for improving education of girls. In Madhya Pradesh under Kanya Saksharta Yojana, SC/ST girls enrolled in class VI were provided an incentive of ₹500. Some states also have fixed deposit schemes and the amount is paid to the girl child on completion of her education.

3.34 The share of socially disadvantaged children (SC/ST) did not show any improvement. However, it was considerably higher than their share in the population due to a large number of overaged children enrolled in the schools. The enrolment share in Himachal Pradesh, Madhya Pradesh and Rajasthan indicate that the majority of the SC/ST children were enrolled in government schools.

3.35 The share of SC/ST teachers in schools was 21%. Madhya Pradesh and Rajasthan which had significant ratios of enrolment of the children of these categories had SC/ST teacher ratios of 39% and 13% respectively. Schools in Haryana had a large share of SC/ST teachers at 63%, West Bengal (30%), Assam (17%), Bihar (17%) as compared to Uttar Pradesh (13%).

3.36 The enrolment of CWSN rose from 0.43% of the total children enrolled in 2003 to 1.17% in 2007 with improved ratios in Assam, Chandigarh and Rajasthan. Under the scheme, Integrated education for Disabled (IED), training was provided to teachers on teaching techniques and for preparation of individualized education plans, children were provided assistive devices such as hearing aids, spectacles, wheelchairs, Braille kits etc. In some states, surgical operations were carried out for children with severe disabilities. Home based education is also provided by some NGOs in Chandigarh. No individualized plans were formulated in all the schools which had CWSN. Retention rates for such children are known to be poor in the absence of supportive academic and school environment. In terms of utilization of funds under IED, Assam, Haryana, Himachal Pradesh and Rajasthan utilized over 90% of their allocation in 2007 on interventions for CWSN whereas Andhra Pradesh (44.4%), Bihar (41.3%) and Chandigarh (27.1%) could not utilize the funds available for IED.

4. QUALITY OF EDUCATION

4.1 In the initial years of SSA, the thrust was on closing the infrastructural gaps as it was recognized that an enabling environment aids learning and can lead to improvement in quality of education imparted by government schools.

4.2 The states were to formulate strategies for improving the quality of education also through recruitment of teachers for ensuring the norm of one teacher for every forty children, expansion of school facilities, provision of free textbooks, regular inservice training to teachers and school grants for repair and maintenance and teaching learning materials.

Infrastructural Facilities

4.3 Most (88%) schools have pucca (all weather) school building. The condition of school buildings was reported to be very poor in Assam as all the schools were more than 20 years old and few schools were functioning from makeshift and temporary (kutcha) buildings. Himachal Pradesh and Tamil Nadu too had a lower percentage of pucca school buildings.

4.4 In the selected samples, 55% of the schools had less than three classrooms and 25% had four to six classrooms. A few had more than six classrooms. Schools in Chandigarh and Haryana have better infrastructure with pucca buildings, boundary walls and more than three classrooms. In some schools without boundary walls in Andhra Pradesh, teachers reported thefts of computers and animal grazing.

4.5 There has been a significant improvement in schools with drinking water facilities for students. 91% of the schools provide drinking water facility either from taps, tubewells, handpumps and stored containers. In Rajasthan 26% of the schools were not providing drinking water and children were visiting their homes during school hours.

4.6 With regard to the availability of common toilets in schools, 82% of the schools had toilet facilities and separate toilets for girls were available in 51% of the schools. As compared to the Northern States/UT of Chandigarh, Haryana and Uttar Pradesh where separate toilets were available in more than 60% of the schools, Andhra Pradesh, Assam, Bihar, Madhya Pradesh and Tamil Nadu had a lower percentage of schools (40%) with separate toilets for girls. Separate toilets for girls in upper primary schools can reduce dropouts, absenteeism and ensure hygiene amongst adolescent girls.

4.7 Few schools in Assam, Bihar, Madhya Pradesh, Rajasthan and Uttar Pradesh are provided with electricity. Even though 77% of schools in Haryana and 70% in Himachal Pradesh had electricity, less than 8% schools in Haryana and 16% in Himachal Pradesh had computer centres in schools. In Bihar, computers had been provided to schools without electricity. The non-availability of trained teachers to impart computer education was also reported as one of the reasons for low computer usage in schools.

Teaching Material and Incentives

4.8 More than 95% of the schools had a blackboard with the exception of a few schools in Himachal Pradesh. The condition of blackboards was reported to be very poor in Bihar. In terms of usage of blackboard by teachers, 96% of the students reported that blackboards were used during teaching.

4.9 The use of Teaching Learning Materials (TLMs) by teachers during teaching enhances interest in learning. All schools in Andhra Pradesh and Madhya Pradesh had TLMs whereas only 8% of the schools in Bihar and 38% of the schools in Haryana and Himachal Pradesh displayed various types of teaching learning material i.e. charts, maps, posters, etc in the classrooms. The most common form of TLMs were charts/posters which were available in 73% of schools while 18% had reading material. Some schools in Assam, Madhya Pradesh and Uttar Pradesh provide educational toys, puzzles and games. Schools in all states except Bihar and Chandigarh (which have only charts/ posters) had a combination of charts, reading material, puzzles and educational toys.

4.10 Students in Andhra Pradesh and Tamil Nadu mentioned that TLMs were used most of the time. However 60% of the students in Chandigarh, Haryana and an equal number in Himachal Pradesh and Madhya Pradesh and 50% in Bihar reported that TLMs were rarely or never used. In Assam, Rajasthan and West Bengal, the responses on usage of TLMs was more than 90%.

4.11 While all teachers are provided grants of ₹500 per year to prepare TLMs, the grants were utilized for purchase of stationary such as books and pencils in Chandigarh and Himachal Pradesh. Teachers reported lack of adequate guidance from the cluster resource centres on the preparation of teaching aids.

4.12 Student responses on the existence of libraries in schools indicated that many schools do not have libraries and reading habits were not being inculcated amongst children. The states where maximum number of students were aware of the existence of libraries was in Andhra Pradesh (94%), Tamil Nadu (87%) and Chandigarh (67%) and the awareness was least in Madhya Pradesh (0.7%).

4.13 Girls and SC/ST children were provided free textbooks under SSA. Non-eligible children were provided free textbooks from state grants/book banks in all states. 84.4% of the students reported that they received textbooks in the beginning of the session. Upper Primary students in Bihar and Himachal Pradesh reported receiving books in the middle and end of the session and some children in upper primary schools in Haryana did not receive the complete set of books. Among the canvassed schools, Girl and SC/ST students in Andhra Pradesh and Tamil Nadu received monetary incentives and few children in Haryana and Rajasthan. In Bihar SC/ST students are provided with scholarships.

School Indicators

4.14 An important indicator of classroom transaction is the Pupil Teacher Ratio. Andhra Pradesh, Chandigarh, Himachal Pradesh and Tamil Nadu had the most number of schools with PTRs less than 40 while schools in Bihar, Uttar Pradesh and West Bengal had high PTRs. With the improved enrolment in the schools, the norm of one teacher for forty children was not maintained as less number of teachers were recruited.

4.15 Madhya Pradesh, Rajasthan and Tamil Nadu had a large number of multi-grade schools. In these states though a number of primary schools were upgraded to upper primary schools or a large number of EGS centres upgraded to primary schools, however schools did not have adequate number of classrooms. 83% of the schools in Madhya Pradesh, 68% of the schools in Rajasthan and 50% of the schools in Tamil Nadu had less than three classrooms. It is evident that children of different grades were being taught in the same classroom. In the short term, teachers should be trained in multi-grade teaching methods and multi-graded books introduced. In the long term construction of additional classrooms will reduce the proportion of multi-graded schools.

4.16 Despite the SSA norms of at least two teachers per school, 7.2% of the schools were single teacher schools and nearly 30% of the schools did not have more than two teachers. Rajasthan (21%), Himachal Pradesh (15%), Haryana (14%), Assam and Uttar Pradesh (12.5%) have the maximum number of single teacher schools.

4.17 Non-availability of adequate number of teacher training institutions has been recognized to be one of the reasons for shortage of teachers in rural areas. At the time of canvassing, 19% of the regular posts of teachers were vacant in schools. The largest number of vacant posts were in Haryana, Madhya Pradesh and Uttar Pradesh though para teachers under SSA were inducted as the recruitment process for such teachers/contract teachers/education volunteers was more liberal and educational qualifications for such teachers were lowered. In Andhra Pradesh, even though teacher vacancies were less than 3%, VECs recruited a large number of para teachers.

Teacher Indicators

4.18 It is widely perceived that better qualified teachers can have a significant effect on quality of education imparted. Nearly 56% of the teachers were graduates with some possessing post graduate qualifications. Schools in Andhra Pradesh, Haryana, Rajasthan and Uttar Pradesh had a high number of graduate teachers compared to schools in Assam, Bihar and Tamil Nadu.

4.19 As part of capacity building for teachers, an induction training of 20 days in a year are provided to new teachers and in service training is also provided. Bihar, Uttar Pradesh and West Bengal had provided training to fewer teachers than other states. It was reported that teachers do not take the training seriously in Himachal Pradesh and that master trainers were not well prepared in Haryana. The feedback from the teachers on the usefulness of the training on the classroom practices needs to be incorporated and training should be re-oriented to include more innovative methods of teaching including multi-graded teaching methods, individualized education plans, sharing of best practices of other states rather than emphasis on quality monitoring, familiarization of new syllabus etc.

4.20 Involvement of teachers in non-teaching activities is rampant with 74% of the teachers involved in election duties, census survey, pulse polio programmes with 54% of the teachers expressing their unwillingness to non-teaching activities. In Andhra Pradesh, Chandigarh, Himachal Pradesh, Madhya Pradesh, Rajasthan and Tamil Nadu fewer teachers were assigned for such duties and were among the most satisfied with their salaries (satisfaction levels of salaries taken as a rough indicator for motivation). It was observed that in Haryana and Uttar Pradesh, more than 90% of the teachers were involved in non-teaching activities with teachers in Uttar Pradesh also involved in supervision of school civil works and cattle survey. The proportion of graduate teachers too was higher in these states and were among the least satisfied with their salaries. Though West Bengal appears as an outlier, teachers should not be utilized for non-teaching activities and ought to be consulted in curriculum design to improve motivation levels.

4.21 Students reported that teachers were regular in Assam, Bihar, Rajasthan and Tamil Nadu. However in Uttar Pradesh and Chandigarh only 88% of the students mentioned that teachers were regular.

4.22 Punishment in any form, physical or verbal abuse generates fear amongst children resulting in poor attendance as well as impacting interest in learning. 26% of the students in Himachal Pradesh mentioned that teachers often resorted to physical punishment. Teachers in Andhra Pradesh Bihar, Chandigarh, Uttar Pradesh and West Bengal also resorted to physical punishment.

4.23 Generally, 84% of the parents of school going children were satisfied with the teachers. The reasons for dissatisfaction were poor quality of teaching (6.52%) in Munger, Muzarffarpur, Purnea (Bihar), Mahendragarh (Haryana) and Jhabua (Madhya Pradesh), teachers remaining absent (3.82%) in Mahboobnagar (Andhra Pradesh), Jhabua (Madhya Pradesh), Muzarffarpur (Bihar) and Chandigarh. A few (2%) disliked that teachers resorted to physical punishment (Andhra Pradesh).

Learning Achievement

4.24 Simple tests based on grade appropriate NCERT curriculum on reading, writing and verbal skills in English, Local Language and Arithmetic were given to students in Class II (primary level). Similarly tests based on reading and writing skills in English, Local language and problem solving tests in Mathematics were designed for Class VI (upper primary students). The question sets were the same for all states and for rural and urban schools.

4.25 Students performance in English and Local Language achievement tests were graded into four categories such as "not at all" (unable to narrate/read or write anything), "poor" (able to narrate up to 40% or write 12 words correctly), "partial" (able to narrate 40-80% or write 13-25 words correctly) and "complete" (ability to narrate more than 80% without any help and write 25 words correctly without any help). In Mathematics, marks were provided for the number of correct questions answered.

4.26 It was observed that quality of education varies across states and age groups. The performance of children in Class II was better in verbal tests as 86% were able to narrate numbers completely, 61% were able to narrate local language alphabets and 60% English alphabets. In reading tests, 42% of the children were able to read local language alphabets correctly, 80% could identify numbers but only 6% could identify English alphabets.

4.27 The results from the written tests in Arithmetic, Local Language and English underlines the fact that the system of education is characterized by rote learning and places less emphasis on writing skills. The average marks in writing tests in Local language and Arithmetic was 54 and that in English was 30.

4.28 The performance of students of Class II in oral, reading and writing tests of local language was comparatively better in Andhra Pradesh, Chandigarh, Tamil Nadu and West Bengal. In Arithmetic too, the performance of students in Andhra Pradesh, Chandigarh, Tamil Nadu and West Bengal was better than their peers in other states. In English, performance of students in writing tests was better in Chandigarh and West Bengal. The performance of students in Class II in Assam, Bihar, Madhya Pradesh, Rajasthan and Uttar Pradesh was lower than the overall average.

4.29 Upper primary level (Class VI) students were tested for passage reading and writing in English and local language. Writing tests included comprehension and essay. In local language tests of reading, 82% were able to read a passage correctly. In English however only 26% were able to read correctly.

4.30 In written tests in English Essay, local language and problem solving in Mathematics, the performance of students in local language was better than English or Mathematics. The gap in performance between English and local language was wide. The performance of students in mathematics was extremely poor, probably due to differences in states' syllabus and the NCERT curriculum.

4.31 The performance of students both at primary and upper primary level was better in Local language than English or Mathematics.

4.32 The performance of students in Class VI in Mathematics was better in Andhra Pradesh, Madhya Pradesh, Tamil

Nadu and West Bengal. In local language and in English, the average marks of students in Chandigarh, Tamil Nadu and West Bengal were better than their counterparts in other states. In Class VI the performance of students in Bihar and Uttar Pradesh was lower than the overall average.

4.33 In general, the performance of students in Andhra Pradesh, Chandigarh, Tamil Nadu and West Bengal indicates that a combination of factors such as teacher availability (average number of teachers per school), better pedagogic practices such as use of TLMs in teaching, access and use of libraries, greater teaching time (less of non-teaching activities) and higher motivation levels improves the quality of education as reflected in the learning outcomes of students.

4.34 Several states have implemented innovative techniques and programmes to improve the quality of teaching. In Andhra Pradesh, schools are graded as "A", "B", "C", "D" based on their performance which improves teacher accountability. In Arunachal Pradesh, "hole in the wall" schools have been opened and computers are provided on the school walls for easy accessibility. Tamil Nadu uses Activity Based Learning cards for children in primary age groups and Activity Learning Methodology for upper primary children. In Haryana and Puducherry EDUSAT facilities have been provided in some primary schools and in block resource centres.

5. FINANCIAL RESOURCES

5.1 As SSA was launched towards the end of the Ninth Five Year Plan (2001-02), the outlay and the expenditure on the scheme was nominal with the total allocation for the programme at ₹ 500 crore only. The total expenditure in 2001-02 incurred by all the states was ₹ 499.9 crore.

5.2 During the Tenth Five Year Plan (2002-2007), the initial total outlay was ₹ 17,000 crore with the centre-state sharing pattern in resources at 75:25. Though the scheme was under-resourced during the first few years of the Tenth Five Year Plan, with the levy of a 2% cess in 2004-05 more resources were earmarked to fund the programme. The expenditure during 2003-04 to 2006-07 as reported by the states was ₹36,367 crore. This may include advances by some of the implementing agencies.

5.3 During the Eleventh Five Year Plan (2007-2012), the outlay is ₹71,000 crore. The centre state sharing pattern is variable during the Plan with 65:35 in the first phase (2007-2009), 60:40 in 2009-2010, 55:45 in 2010-2011 and 50:50 in 2011-2012. The Northeastern States have a special dispensation that the centre-state ratio would be 90:10. During the first two years of the Eleventh Plan, the expenditure on the programme was reported to be ₹24,136 crore.

Centre-State Shares

5.4 The Sarva Shiksha Abhiyan programme is based on the premise that financing of elementary education interventions has to be sustainable. In 2007, 22 of the 35 States (and UTs) were able to maintain the funding patterns as envisaged in the Tenth Five Year Plan. With the exception of Andaman and Nicobar Islands, Arunachal Pradesh and Punjab, all the remaining states were able to raise more resources in nominal terms in 2007 than in 2003.

5.5 The total allocation for the programme steadily increased from ₹8,371 crore in 2003-04 to ₹20,691 crore in 2006-07. With the increase in allocation, assistance to state implementing societies by way of releases of central and the state share also increased significantly. In 2003-04 assistance was 43.17% of the allocation which rose to 73.06% of the allocation in 2006-07. Central assistance as percentage of allocation declined in relative terms in the case of Gujarat and Kerala while state assistance as a percentage of allocation declined in Andhra Pradesh, Assam, Karnataka and Tamil Nadu.

Release of Funds

5.6 It was observed that though more funds were released by the states to the implementing societies, the disbursements by the state implementing societies to the districts declined from 109% in 2003-04 to 96% in 2006-07. States/UTs which disbursed more than 98% of the assistance in 2006-07 were Andhra Pradesh, Bihar, Chandigarh, Daman & Diu, Dadra Nagar Haveli, Goa, Gujarat, Himachal Pradesh, Jharkhand, Kerala, Maharashtra, Meghalaya, Nagaland, Orissa, Puducherry, Rajasthan, Uttar Pradesh and West Bengal. A small portion of the funds were utilized by the state implementing societies in some states for purchase of textbooks, computers etc and sometimes retained due to the untimely receipt of utilization certificates from the districts.

Utilisation of Funds

5.7 The utilisation ratio at state level (expenditure to assistance) increased from 98% in 2003-04 to 110% in 2006-07 indicating better absorptive capacity. Expenditures were reported to be higher as unspent balances in the previous years were also utilized. As against 13 states which were able to utilize more than 100% of the funds (including unspent balances of previous years) in 2003-04,19 states including UTs were able to utilize more than 100% in 2006-07. Thus in terms of the expenditure on available funds, there was an improvement in 2006-07.

5.8 States which utilized more than 90% of the allocation in 2006-07 were Arunachal Pradesh, Jammu and Kashmir, Karnataka, Maharashtra, Nagaland and Tripura. Assam, Puducherry and West Bengal reported poor utilization of funds due to delay in receipt of funds possibly on account of late submission of utilization certificates.

5.9 It was observed that Daman Diu, Goa, Gujarat, Kerala and Manipur spent a higher proportion of the funds on quality interventions such as teacher training, innovative activities, teacher grant etc than other states. Andaman Nicobar Islands, Bihar, Punjab and West Bengal spent 60% of the total expenditure on civil works and maintenance. Chandigarh, Chhattisgarh and Puducherry spent more relatively on administration such as MIS and management, community training etc.

Disbursements of Funds to the Districts

5.10 There was an improvement in the flow of funds as districts except Haryana, Himachal Pradesh and Nadia (West Bengal) reported that they received their first instalment of funds between April to May as compared to September-December in the early years of SSA. In Himachal Pradesh and Haryana, delays were reported in the receipt of first instalment (June/July/August) and Nadia district (West Bengal) reported that they received the first instalment only in August/September. Though the time gap for transfer from the districts to the blocks was only a month the transfer from the block to the VECs (Village Education Committees) varies with some states making monthly disbursements and some transferring the second instalment as late as March.

5.11 The disbursements to the districts was not based on any criteria of educational backwardness/low female literacy or higher percentage of socially disadvantaged groups (tribal areas) but on the number of schools, unspent balances, utilization etc. In Andhra Pradesh, Uttar Pradesh and West Bengal, districts with more number of educationally backward blocks were disbursed less funds than other districts with less number of backward blocks. In 2003-04, East Godavari district (Andhra Pradesh) which has only one backward block received ₹29.5 crore as compared to Chittoor with 20 backward blocks which received ₹15.09 crore. Nadia (West Bengal) which has no backward block received ₹42.04 crore whereas Siliguri which has two backward blocks received ₹12.2 crore. The low prioritisation for educationally backward areas continued in 2007 though the differences in the allocations between the districts had narrowed. Further, district authorities in Nadia reported that the flow of funds from the State was irregular. Lack of flexibility to the district authorities to reallocate resources between heads was reported from Haryana and Nadia (West Bengal).

Utilisation of Funds at District Level

5.12 Utilization of funds at the district level in the selected samples too improved in 2006-07 as compared to 2003-04. As against fourteen districts which reported expenditure of more than 100% (use of unspent balances), twenty three districts reported expenditures of more than 100% in 2006-07. Further, in comparison to seven districts which spent less than 80% in 2003-2004, only two districts spent less than 80% in 2006-07.

5.13 It was observed that in the selected districts, expenditures matched the funds released and in a few cases, unspent funds, interest earned on deposits were also utilized. Most district authorities did not report any inadequacy of funds except Chittoor and Kurnool in Andhra Pradesh, Jorhat, Kamrup, Morigaon in Assam, Pune in Maharashtra, Karaikal (Puducherry) and Kanyakumari in Tamil Nadu and Nadia, Burdwan in West Bengal.

Expenditure on Interventions

5.14 In terms of utilization of funds against the budgeted outlays (allocation), the maximum share of funds were spent on "Civil Works" and "Repair and Maintenance". The average utilization on these two components relative to allocation was 92%. Utilisation on computer education (50%), innovative activities for improving quality (54%)

and teachers training (67%) were lower indicating that districts were unable to utilize the funds on interventions as planned.

5.15 The share of civil works and repair and maintenance in total expenditures in 2006-07 was 77% as compared to expenditures on Quality interventions (6.21%) comprising teachers' grant, teacher learning material, teachers training and teaching learning equipment.

School Level Grants and Expenditure

5.16 With the increase in grants, the unevenness in the distribution of funds amongst schools was reduced with more schools provided with grants in 2006-2007. The number of schools that did not receive grants declined from 17% in 2003-04 to 7% in 2006-07 and the funds allocated increased by more than six times. In Andhra Pradesh, primary and upper primary schools continued to receive a fixed amount of ₹2,000-3,000 per year during the reference period. In Assam, the average amount allocated per school in 2007 was ₹7,000 per year. In Andhra Pradesh and Assam, upper primary schools received almost the same outlays as much as primary schools.

5.17 All government schools are provided with school grants, teacher grants and funds for civil works. More than 95% of the schools were able to utilize completely the grants provided to them except in Bihar, a few in Uttar Pradesh which were unable to utilise the grants as they did not receive it in time or the sanction for work was not available. Government-aided schools in rented buildings do not receive funds for repair and maintenance. At school level, excluding teacher salaries, the average expenditure incurred per student per year improved from ₹94 in 2003-04 to ₹497 in 2006-07. Expenditures of more than ₹500 per student per year were incurred in Assam (₹678), Bihar (₹910), Haryana (₹738), Madhya Pradesh (₹663) and Uttar Pradesh (₹538). The lowest spending was reported from

Andhra Pradesh. The average expenditures in Bihar were higher due to the large expenditures on civil works.

5.18 As the expenditures incurred by the sampled schools are funded entirely by the grants of the government (centre and the state), there appears to be a need for improved spending on elementary education in Andhra Pradesh, Chandigarh, Himachal Pradesh, Rajasthan, Tamil Nadu and West Bengal.

6. COMMUNITY OWNERSHIP AND ROLE OF DEVELOPMENT PARTNERS

Community Participation

One of the salient features of the SSA is its emphasis on decentralized implementation. The programme calls for community ownership of school based interventions by involvement of Women's groups, Village Education Committee members, Mother Teacher Associations/Parent Teacher Associations and members of Panchayati Raj institutions.

Activities of Village Education Committees

6.1 The Village Education Committees (VECs) have an essential role in monitoring and supervision of schools, appointment of para teachers, mainstreaming dropouts by carrying out campaigns, generating awareness for improving enrolment besides repair and maintenance of schools. To empower these decentralized bodies funds for upgradation, maintenance, repair of schools and Teaching Learning equipment are transferred to VECs/equivalent bodies such as school management committees/gram panchayat or any other school level arrangement for decentralized implementation.

6.2 In the selected villages 80% of the VECs were involved in civil work including repair and maintenance related activities in schools. In Assam, Bihar, Chandigarh, Haryana and Rajasthan VECs were predominantly involved in infrastructure improvement and management of funds. In Chandigarh their functioning is reportedly limited to the issue of grants for school improvement.

6.3 VECs have been effective in improving enrolment and in reducing out of school children by carrying out enrolment drives, organizing awareness campaigns. In Madhya Pradesh, school management committees are involved in implementation of SSA interventions at the grassroot level.

6.4 In monitoring and supervision of schools i.e., monitoring teacher and student absenteeism, availability of books etc, SECs in Madhya Pradesh and VECs in Rajasthan and Uttar Pradesh were the least active compared to the VECs in Assam, Andhra Pradesh, Bihar, Chandigarh, Tamil Nadu and West Bengal.

6.5 To overcome the shortage of teachers VECs were empowered to appoint para teachers. VECs in Andhra Pradesh were the most involved as has been observed in the appointment of para teachers in the schools. Only 8% of the VECs in Bihar and 25% in Himachal Pradesh and Haryana claimed to have appointed teachers.

6.6 Though all schools in Bihar maintain records of children enrolled in schools, very few VECs maintain records of fund receipt and utilization. The records of the meetings conducted by VECs indicate that periodicity of the meetings were not fixed. In Bihar, Madhya Pradesh, Rajasthan and Uttar Pradesh, meetings were reportedly held on monthly basis. In Himachal Pradesh and Tamil Nadu, VECs were ineffective as regular meetings were not being held.

6.7 The major issues discussed in the meetings pertained to delay in receipt of funds, infrastructure issues pertaining to poor construction of buildings, lack of toilets, furniture in schools, shortage of teachers/absenteeism, students' attendance and timely availability of books.

6.8 All the village committees in Tamil Nadu were most concerned about infrastructure issues such as shortage of classrooms, drinking water and toilet facilities in schools. Inadequate funds and/or delay in receipt of funds were major issues in the village meetings in Himachal Pradesh, Madhya Pradesh and Tamil Nadu, student absenteeism a major concern in Assam, Bihar, Madhya Pradesh, Rajasthan and Uttar Pradesh, whereas teachers shortage/absenteeism were major matters in Assam and Madhya Pradesh. Since fund matters is the predominant issue in VECs meetings, quarterly disbursements from the block to the VECs may need to be considered. VECs also need to be provided with funds for appointment of para teachers, sweepers/security staff in schools.

6.9 The capacity building of VEC members is undertaken by the block resource centres as they are the vital intermediaries between the schools and the implementing agencies. The VEC members are sensitized about interventions under SSA, on their role as development partners, organization of mobilization campaigns, school management, civil works etc., to improve their participation in the school ownership system. The training is provided to eight to ten community and women members of the VEC for a period of two/three days in a year. The majority of the members in Assam, Bihar, Rajasthan and Tamil Nadu underwent training.

6.10 Assam, Himachal Pradesh, Madhya Pradesh and Rajasthan spent more than 95% of the allocation on training for community members in 2006-07. Chandigarh spent less than 16%, though training was not conducted for any of the members in the selected villages. Bihar could utilize only 56% while Uttar Pradesh spent 89% of its allocation. The fact that few schools in the selected villages (except in Assam and Himachal Pradesh) displayed the receipt of funds or attendance of teachers on the notice board and the non-maintenance of records suggests that the training of VEC members fell short of inculcating a sense of responsibility and ownership which needs to be strengthened through involvement of parents and awareness generation through NGOs.

6.11 VECs in turn impart training to parents/mothers/ community leaders over a period of one or two days for 7-10 members every year. None of the VECs had imparted any training to its members in Chandigarh and Rajasthan.

Parents Teachers Associations

6.12 Parents Teachers Associations, the primary stakeholders can play a prominent role in the overall governance of school education. However, only 50% of the parents were aware of PTA/MTAs in schools. Even though parents were regular visitors to the schools as none of the schools display the list of members of PTAs, awareness regarding the existence of these associations was poor except in Andhra Pradesh, Bihar, Madhya Pradesh, Tamil Nadu and West Bengal. In these states, parents were reported to be involved in supervision of meals and provided assistance in teaching.

6.13 In Uttar Pradesh, fewer parents were aware of PTAs/ SSA and were not inclined in becoming members of the PTAs. In Chandigarh and Haryana too, the awareness of PTA and SSA was lower than in other states. States in which parents reported lower awareness of PTAs also reported poor awareness of SSA interventions.

6.14 Awareness regarding SSA interventions were better in Assam and Tamil Nadu which probably led to the lower incidence of out of school children. In Bihar, even though awareness of PTA/SSA was reported to be high, enrolment drives had not been conducted in the recent years. In Rajasthan, Madhya Pradesh and West Bengal too, fewer parents could recall that enrolment drives had been conducted. With average awareness about PTA and SSA being only 50% and 55% respectively and membership being as low as 16%, PTAs need to be made more effective. VECs in these states must make efforts to conduct awareness campaigns as well as organise enrolment drives for out of school children.

6.15 In terms of the involvement of the community, the participation of VECs is apparently far better than the involvement of parents associations across most states. In Assam and Bihar, parents as well as the VECs were actively involved in school affairs whereas in Chandigarh, Haryana, Himachal Pradesh, Rajasthan and Uttar Pradesh, the involvement of parents in school activities needs to be encouraged.

Participation by NGOs

6.16 The involvement of NGOs at the grassroots level has been crucial for extending the reach of the interventions specifically in the area of inclusive education for disabled by supporting initiatives for identification, medical/health check up camps, home education, sensitizing teachers as also to schools in providing assistance in teaching, quality improvement techniques, material supplies, teaching aids and assessing student performance. NGOs were involved in implementation of SSA in all the selected districts except Baran, Goalpara, Jalore, Kanpur Dehat, Munger, Muzaffarpur and Morigaon. AIE centres were operated by NGOs in Haryana, Madhya Pradesh, Maharashtra, Tamil Nadu and West Bengal. Andhra Pradesh has encouraged some industrial houses and well known NGOs' to adopt schools, in setting up of EGS/AIE centres for mainstreaming dropouts and providing computer education.

Block and Cluster Resource Centres

6.17 The Block resource centres have been set up in every block headquarter to provide teacher assistance, organising seminars and teacher training, syllabus designing, distribution of textbooks, monitor the performance of the schools, receive funds from the district authorities and distribute it amongst schools. Block resource centres were functional in all blocks except in Mayong and Kapili (Assam). In Khoribari (West Bengal), the BRC (CLRC) was reported to be non-functional with the VECs receiving the funds directly from the district authorities.

6.18 Cluster resource centres have been set up at the sub block levels. However 77% of the block resource centres and 45% of the cluster resource centres were located more than 3 kilometres from the schools. Andhra Pradesh, Bihar and Rajasthan had the most number of CRCs located at far distances from the schools.

6.19 All the respondents were aware of the existence of BRCs and CRCs in Andhra Pradesh, Haryana, Madhya Pradesh, Uttar Pradesh and West Bengal. The coordination between CRCs and school headmasters was weak in Assam, Chandigarh and Himachal Pradesh. In Assam, too many schools in the catchment area of each CRC impacted effective academic guidance, in Chandigarh, most CRCs were located at far distances. In Himachal Pradesh, though there were more number of CRCs, the school headmasters reported that there had been no visits of BRC or CRC members in several years as the Block Education officers had dual responsibilities of the implementation of SSA as well as state schemes. While Block resource centre officials mentioned that they held monthly meetings there was no system of maintaining records of visits of BRCs/CRCs to schools. The functioning of the BRCs was reportedly better than the CRCs in most blocks.

6.20 Staff constraints (Himachal Pradesh, West Bengal), poor infrastructure (Chandigarh, Siliguri), a tight budget for contingency funds and the distance from the schools results in weak linkages in monitoring and supervision. Duties and performance indicators for cluster resource centre personnel should also be clearly specified so as to ensure statutory accountability. CRCs need to be revitalized for providing academic support, guidance in the preparation of TLMs, monitoring quality and teacher and student attendance.

Monitoring Systems

6.21 The monitoring systems under SSA envisage the constitution of state level, district level and block level monitoring committees. State level monitoring committees have been constituted in all states except in Goa, Jammu and Kashmir, Meghalaya, Nagaland, Orissa, Sikkim, Uttar Pradesh and in UTs such as Chandigarh, Dadra and Nagar Haveli, Lakshadweep and Puducherry. The state teams were reportedly meeting regularly and involved in monitoring the implementation of all SSA interventions and civil works. The monitoring team in Rajasthan had also carried out inspection of schools.

6.22 District level monitoring teams had been constituted in all the districts but the norms governing the composition of teams, their functions and frequency of visits were not clear. The main activity of most district teams were monitoring schools. School mapping was carried out only in one district of Assam, one in Uttar Pradesh and in all the districts in Tamil Nadu. As most district educational officers hold multiple charges (SSA as well as other state schemes), there is lack of time and attention to SSA interventions. All the district teams in Tamil Nadu were reported to be effective.

6.23 In thirteen districts (44%), meetings were reported to be conducted on monthly basis, fortnightly meetings were reported to be conducted in six districts, weekly meetings in six other districts, only quarterly in Baran district and on half yearly basis in Ujjain and Mahendragarh.

6.24 Block level teams had been constituted in all blocks except Mahendragarh (Haryana), Chamba and Baijhari (Himachal Pradesh). After, Thandla and Alirajpur (Madhya Pradesh) and in Haringhata (one of the two blocks), Matigara and Khoribari (West Bengal). The frequency of meetings/monitoring of activities was claimed to be rather regular with 55% of the monitoring teams meeting on monthly basis. While there were no NGOs assisting monitoring teams in Andhra Pradesh, in Chandigarh and in Tamil Nadu they were involved in monitoring in the selected districts.

6.25 Community participation and parents' involvement are vital for effecting better linkages with support centres. Monitoring activities (school mapping and achievement) of district level monitoring teams need to be strengthened.

7. URBAN FINDINGS

7.1 For the purpose of assessing the implementation of SSA in towns, urban samples were also selected.

Selection Criteria

7.2 From each zone, one state with highest slum population was selected and two towns were selected from that state. Two towns from Puducherry (UT) were also selected. Two slums were selected from each selected town. Though 12 towns and 24 slums were selected from five states and one UT for the study, however 13 towns and 22 slums were actually canvassed.

Accessibility

7.3 Though 93% of children in slums access neighbourhood elementary schools which are within walking distance (1 km) from the slum more than half do not have access to schools within slums. A few children in Hyderabad and Navi Mumbai travel more than 1 km from their slums to reach their schools.

7.4 The government and government-aided schools under the management of the town local body (Municipal Corporation) constitute around 78% of the educational facilities in urban slum areas. In towns of Karaikal and

Ozhukarai in Puducherry and in Agra and Kanpur Nagar in Uttar Pradesh, government schools were predominant whereas in towns of Hyderabad and Yemmiganur in Andhra Pradesh, Jorhat in Assam, Pune and Navi Mumbai in Maharashtra, there were schools under the management of the municipal corporation. In Kolkata and Burdwan, there was a predominance of government-aided schools.

Underserved Slums

7.5 In terms of accessibility to upper primary schools, students in slums were able to access upper primary schools in their neighbourhood in Hyderabad and Yemmiganur (Andhra Pradesh) as well as in Pune and Navi Mumbai (Maharashtra). In Assam and Puducherry, upper primary schools were available in only one of the four slums. In West Bengal, it was reported that none of the slums canvassed had upper primary schools in their neighbourhood. It was also observed that except in Andhra Pradesh and Maharashtra, no new schools were opened for slum children within the last ten years. Except Andhra Pradesh and Maharashtra, the urban slums are underserved in terms of the availability of upper primary schools in close proximity to the slums.

Enrolment and Attendance

7.6 Despite the presence of private schools, enrolment in government schools and schools operated by Municipal corporations (local governing bodies) increased substantially by 18% especially in Andhra Pradesh and Maharashtra. Enrolment also improved in West Bengal in government and government-aided schools. Free books, midday meals and availability of multilingual schools in towns as in Maharashtra contributed to improved enrolment ratios.

7.7 In the selected schools, 68% of the schools reported student attendance of more than 75%. Student absenteeism was high in Uttar Pradesh while all schools in Puducherry reported 100% attendance. The reasons for absenteeism in schools in Maharashtra, Uttar Pradesh and West Bengal were "work at home", ill health and taking care of siblings.

Out of School Children

7.8 The largest number of out of school children were in the slum households in Pune, Kanpur, Agra and Kolkata. In the selected samples, 20% of the slum households had children who were out of school. The poor economic condition of the migrants, lack of parental attention, use of child labour in households and commercial establishments were the main causes for children remaining out of school.

7.9 More than half of the out of school children belong to socially disadvantaged groups (SC/STs). While Uttar Pradesh had the majority of out of school children in the selected samples, 70% of these children in Maharashtra were girls. It is observed that pre-primary sections in primary schools were non-existent in Uttar Pradesh or few in Andhra Pradesh and West Bengal. Better availability of pre-primary sections/upper primary schools/NPEGEL schools within the neighbourhood of the slums could lead to a significant reduction in the number of girls dropping out of schools.

7.10 Financial incentives and uniforms need to be provided to slum children to improve enrolment. 84% of the out of school children were willing to attend schools and their expectations were free uniforms, textbooks and scholarships. Greater awareness needs to be generated as 55% of the parents were unaware of SSA interventions.

Gender and Social Gaps

7.11 There was a substantial improvement in enrolment of girls resulting in gender parity ratio of 0.82 in 2007. While Assam and Puducherry achieved gender parity, Andhra Pradesh and Maharashtra reported a significant rise in enrolment of girls resulting in improved gender parity ratios.

7.12 The share of socially disadvantaged groups in school enrolment remained stagnant (30%) with large variations between states. In Maharashtra, the improvement in overall enrolment resulted in improved gender and social parity ratio. In West Bengal, overall enrolment increased by 43%, but share of girls' enrolment and of SC/STs declined and in Uttar Pradesh, the decline in enrolment also resulted in decline in gender parity.

7.13 The share of differently-abled children in school enrolment declined. Slum schools in Assam, Puducherry and Uttar Pradesh reportedly did not provide any incentives to students and there were no ramps in schools. Only a few schools had individualised education plans or had provided incentives. In Uttar Pradesh, though it was claimed that funds had been spent on IED, it was reported that none of the disabled children had received any incentives in the selected schools.

Infrastructural Facilities

7.14 The availability of infrastructure in urban slum schools indicates that though 93% of the schools were located in pucca (all weather) buildings, these are often in rented premises and do not receive repair and maintenance grant. In Assam and West Bengal, only 50% of the schools had boundary walls. Thefts of fans and roof (asbestos sheets) were reported from one of the schools in Navi Mumbai and use of school toilets by slum people from Yemmiganur. Few schools had facilities for playground but limited space for activities within the classrooms. The limited area in the schools leaves no scope for construction of ramps to make schools disabled friendly.

7.15 Drinking water facilities were available in 82% of the schools except some schools in Yemmiganur (Andhra Pradesh), in Kolkata (West Bengal) and due to non-functional handpumps in Uttar Pradesh. Water from stored containers were provided in Andhra Pradesh and Puducherry, from tubewells in Jorhat and handpumps in Kanpur and Agra. Though toilets were available in 82% of the schools, separate toilets for girls were available in only 40% of the schools. None of the selected schools in West Bengal had toilets for girls. The sanitation facilities in urban slum schools were in neglect and funds for maintenance need to be provided to improve school environment.

7.16 In 86% of urban slum schools electricity was available. Though all the selected slum schools in Maharashtra, Puducherry and West Bengal had electricity in schools, computers were not provided to any of the schools in West Bengal and were available in only one school in Puducherry and three schools in Maharashtra.

School Indicators

7.17 As per computed pupil teacher ratio, 57% of the schools had PTR ratios of less than 40. In Uttar Pradesh, it was reported that two government primary schools had PTR ratios of 70 and 107.

7.18 The increase in enrolment led to high PTR ratios in all the schools in Maharashtra. Though all schools had upper primary sections, they operate in double shifts resulting in few or no multi-grade classes. The enrolment in schools in Andhra Pradesh too improved substantially, PTRs were high (50% of the schools have PTRs of more than 40) and as some schools have few classrooms (1-3 classrooms), 75% of the schools had multi-grade classes. Primary schools in West Bengal too had multi-grade classes. In Uttar Pradesh, PTRs were very high despite the fact that para teachers had been appointed under SSA. To improve PTR ratios, teachers need to be appointed and schools should operate double shifts. Teachers should be trained in multi-graded teaching techniques to improve the quality of education in these schools.

7.19 Teacher vacancy positions in 2007 (during the period of canvassing), were high in Uttar Pradesh and West Bengal as recruitment of new teachers had not taken place for several years in these states. However under SSA, para teachers were appointed in all schools. In the urban towns in Andhra Pradesh, more para teachers had been appointed than in other towns.

7.20 The proportion of female teachers in Puducherry was closest to the desirable norm of 50% of female teachers in schools. In Andhra Pradesh and Maharashtra, share of girls' enrolment increased despite the low proportion of female teachers in schools.

7.21 Schools in Puducherry, Maharashtra and Uttar Pradesh had fewer graduate teachers which reflects the lack of interest amongst qualified people to take up teaching jobs in government schools. However teacher availability position was better in Puducherry and Maharashtra, with an average of 11 and 16 teachers per school respectively.

7.22 In service teacher training and induction training had been organized by the town authorities. In Maharashtra only 74% of the teachers were provided in service training whereas in Puducherry 90.1% of the teachers had attended in service training.

7.23 In 75% of the schools, teachers were involved in non-teaching activities such as census survey and election duties. In Assam, fewer teachers were involved with non-teaching activities and were among the most satisfied with their level of salaries. In Maharashtra and Uttar Pradesh, teachers in all the schools were engaged in non-teaching activities, the least interested in performing non-teaching activities and among the least satisfied. In Puducherry, though teachers were involved in non-teaching activities, 50% of the schools reported that teachers were consulted in curriculum design. In general, teachers who are not assigned any non-teaching activity or are consulted in preparation of school education plans can be expected to report higher levels of satisfaction. Higher motivation level of teachers can contribute to improvement in the quality of teaching.

Teaching Learning Material and Incentives

7.24 All girl students and SC/ST children were provided free textbooks. Other non-eligible children were provided free textbooks from state grants or through book banks. 98% of the students received their textbooks in the beginning of the session and with some delays in Andhra Pradesh and Maharashtra reportedly due to the unanticipated increase in enrolment in these states.

7.25 Teaching Learning materials were available in 93% of the urban slum schools. Only one school in Navi Mumbai and one school in Kolkata did not have any TLMs. As per students perception, 91% reported that TLMs were used frequently by the teachers. TLMs were frequently used for teaching by teachers in Puducherry and the least utilized in Uttar Pradesh.

7.26 Though 66% of the schools had libraries, only 35% of the students were utilising them. Reading habits were better amongst students in Andhra Pradesh as 71% of the students made use of the libraries. In Puducherry, 75% of the schools had library facilities but were not utilised by the students. Earmarking of funds for purchase of library books and greater access to libraries can improve reading habits.

7.27 Incentives in the form of scholarships were provided to SC/ST girls in Puducherry and Uttar Pradesh and to meritorious SC/ST girl students in Navi Mumbai. Midday meals were provided to all students in all schools except two schools in Assam and one school in Kolkata. The Education Department in Puducherry was reportedly providing breakfast, noon meal, note books, uniforms, raincoats, stationery to students to improve retention.

7.28 Students reported that teachers were regular, though in Uttar Pradesh and West Bengal the percentages were lower than the overall average. All the students in Puducherry, 18.7% of students in Uttar Pradesh and 3.23% in West Bengal also reported being physically punished by their teachers frequently.

Learning Achievement

7.29 In the selected schools, the percentage of children who had been retained in classes I and II was high except Uttar Pradesh. Though it was reported in West Bengal that the state follows a policy of no detention in primary classes, children had been retained in primary classes in urban schools. Since most of the slum children are first generation learners with poor educational backgrounds, a no failure policy can provide a supportive learning environment and improve retention.

7.30 Primary and upper primary students in the selected schools were tested in verbal, reading and writing skills in English, Local language, and Arithmetic. In tests of verbal ability, the performance of children in primary classes (Class II) to narrate numbers, English alphabets and local language alphabets was better than their rural counterparts. 65% of the students were able to narrate English alphabets correctly, 80% could narrate the alphabets in local language correctly and 95% of the students could narrate numbers 1-20 in the local language completely.

7.31 The performance of students of class II in reading tests in local language revealed that 58% were able to read more than 80% of the words correctly. In English only 7% were able to read more than 80% words correctly and 88% were able to identify numbers correctly. State-wise performance in local language reading tests revealed better performance by students in Puducherry (100%) and Maharashtra (69%). In identification of numbers, the performance was better in Assam (100%), Maharashtra (94%), Puducherry (93%) and Andhra Pradesh (92%).

7.32 The results from the written tests in Arithmetic, English and local language revealed that the students were able to perform better in their own mother tongue than in English. The average marks in local language, Arithmetic and English was 74, 69 and 35 respectively. The coefficient of variation indicates that performance of students in Assam, Puducherry, Maharashtra and West Bengal were better than the overall average.

7.33 In achievement test for class VI (upper primary), 87% of the students were able to read passages correctly in local language in comparison to 16% in English. Students in Maharashtra (38%) and Puducherry (25%) did well in English Passage reading than the overall average. In passage reading skills in local language performance of students in Maharashtra (100%) and Assam (88%) was better than the overall average.

7.34 In writing tests of English and local language and problem solving in Mathematics, the performance of the students in local language was better than English and Mathematics.

7.35 Across states, performance of primary students in Andhra Pradesh, Puducherry, Maharashtra and West Bengal (Class II) and of upper primary students in Assam, Puducherry and Maharashtra was better than other states. Though no single factor could be identified for the superior performance of students in some states, the availability of teachers (more teachers per school, low vacancies) and use of TLMs in teaching appears to impact learning outcomes in government schools.

Implementing Agencies

7.36 The nodal agency for implementation of SSA is the Education Department in Hyderabad, Secunderabad, Yemmiganur (Andhra Pradesh), Guwahati and Jorhat (Assam), Karaikal and Ozhukarai (Puducherry) and Agra City (Uttar Pradesh). In Pune, Navi Mumbai (Maharashtra) and in Kolkata, Raniganj (West Bengal), the scheme is implemented through Municipal corporations and in Kanpur through the Slum Development Authority.

7.37 The funds for implementation of the SSA interventions were transferred by the state implementing societies directly to the Municipal Corporations for schools under its management and to the School Management Committee in aided schools, the School Management Committees in Guwahati and Slum Education Committee in Jorhat and Puducherry. There was no involvement of the District project office in transfer of funds or in coordinating the activities of the different Municipal Corporations within the towns.

Town Committees

7.38 Town committees were assigned the task of conducting training programmes for teachers, community members in wards/slums, monitor the performance of schools, organize awareness campaigns and coordinate with urban resource centres and cluster resource centres. Training for teachers and community members were conducted in Agra City, Guwahati, Pune, Navi Mumbai and Raniganj but not in Andhra Pradesh, Jorhat, Kolkata, Kanpur and Karaikal. Though Karaikal is a separate town, the town level committee in Puducherry was implementing the SSA interventions.

7.39 Town monitoring committees in Agra City, Kanpur Nagar and Puducherry reported that meetings with WECs/ SECs/schools on issues related to funds, enrolment of dropouts were held regularly on monthly basis whereas only annually in Pune and Navi Mumbai. In other towns there was no record of meetings held with WECs or school management committees.

7.40 For mainstreaming dropouts in urban areas, the town authorities in Hyderabad had organised vocational courses for girls, bridge courses of short duration, mobile learning centres and arranged for distance education programmes. In Puducherry, night schools had been opened for slow learners and in Maharashtra, enrolment drives and bridge courses had been conducted. In Jorhat, "Jyoti Kendras" were set up to mainstream out of school children. NPEGEL schemes or AIE centres were not in operation in any of the slums.

Slum Committees

7.41 The Slum/Ward/School Education Committees were reported to be effective with greater involvement in monitoring SSA interventions, school infrastructure improvement, in seeking funds, organizing awareness campaigns for enrolling children in the slums etc. In comparison, the town committees were constrained by lack of interest of the officials (Councillors/Corporators) and non-existence of plans for schools in urban slums.

7.42 The slum level committees in Puducherry were most effective as they held monthly meetings, conducted door to door campaigns for enrolling children and reducing out of school children, training had been provided to the community members and also maintained data on enrolment. WECs in Assam, Maharashtra and slum committees in West Bengal were partially effective. The major constraints faced by the slum committees pertained to shortage or delay in receipt of funds resulting in poor condition of school infrastructure.

School Funds

7.43 As all schools in the slums in Puducherry and Uttar Pradesh are government schools, grants for civil works, maintenance and repair were provided from SSA funds. In Maharashtra and West Bengal, government-aided schools in rented buildings did not receive grants for civil works or maintenance.

7.44 There was an overall improvement in the allocation and utilization of school funds. All schools were able to utilize more than 95% of the grants released to them in 2006-07. The poor utilization of funds in Puducherry was due to the delay in receipt of funds. The marginal improvement in the grants available to the schools in 2007 reflects the fact that the majority of funds were disbursed to schools in the rural areas.

7.45 The indicative average expenditure incurred on students revealed wide differences amongst states. In Maharashtra the town authorities reported that funds provided to schools were not adequate.

Parents Teachers Associations

7.46 School level officials reported that PTA/MTAs had been constituted in all the schools and parents assist school authorities in meal preparation, in distribution and render assistance in teaching. However, awareness amongst parents regarding the functioning/existence of PTAs and MTAs was only 45%. In Yemmiganur, it was reported that school management committees and PTAs had been disbanded. Greater awareness of SSA interventions as in Assam and Puducherry led to the lower incidence of dropouts in these towns.

7.47 NGOs were reportedly involved in setting up of AIE centres, conducting learning enhancement programmes, implementing IED programmes for CWSN children in Pune, Navi Mumbai, Hyderabad and Raniganj, though no NGO was functioning in any of the selected slums. In other towns their presence was reported to be negligible.

Urban and Cluster Resource Centres

7.48 Institutions such as the Urban Resource Centres equivalent of block resource centres were existent and functional in Agra, Guwahati, Pune, Navi Mumbai, Raniganj and Secunderabad and engaged in conducting survey/ awareness campaigns and enrolling CWSN children. The URCs were not maintaining any data on the number of children enrolled in schools.

7.49 Cluster Resource Centres have been set up in the towns. 71.4% of the respondents (School headmasters) were aware of the existence of CRCs. 10% of the CRCs were within school premises and 80% within 3 kms. In Assam and Maharashtra, two CRCs were reported to be located more than 3 kms from the schools. Only few schools had received academic support and 65% reported that CRCs had provided training to teachers. CRCs in Assam and Uttar Pradesh were also involved in monitoring and in textbook distribution in Maharashtra. Though all the CRCs in Puducherry were located within 3 kms, none of them had provided academic support to the schools.

7.50 Given the tough socioeconomic condition in the slums, a cramped living environment and poor sanitation facilities, it is necessary to provide a congenial environment in schools by earmarking funds for repair and maintenance in government-aided schools functioning from rented buildings. Since the district authorities have limited jurisdiction over Municipal schools, there is no nodal agency for monitoring the implementation of SSA in municipal and government-aided schools in the towns. A separate nodal agency needs to be constituted for monitoring the activities of the schools in the urban slums with separate plans that provides for scholarships, uniforms to all children living and attending schools in slum areas, setting up of education monitoring committees at slum level and NPEGEL schemes and vocational schools in every cluster. CRCs need to be set up in Andhra Pradesh and Uttar Pradesh and in general need to be strengthened for more effective exchange with teachers and entrusted with providing academic guidance, organizing awareness camps along with enrolment drives.

8. CONSTRAINTS IN IMPLEMENTATION

Shortage of Teachers/Absenteeism

1. Teacher vacancies were high at 19% in rural schools and 12% in the urban schools (at the time of canvassing). While some states such as Uttar Pradesh and West Bengal had not recruited regular teachers for several

years (due to court cases, weak state finances), lack of adequate number of teacher training institutions in rural areas was reported to be one of the reasons for teacher shortages.

2. Teacher motivation is low on account of non-teaching activities such as pulse polio, supervision of civil works, household surveys. Teachers are not consulted in curriculum construction or in the preparation of district education plans.
3. Teachers are unwilling to be posted to remote areas.
4. Separate teachers for Maths/science/computers are not available.

Inadequate Support Manpower

1. No separate/permanent staff for SSA implementation at district and sub district levels. Most district level staff (in Assam, Bihar, Haryana, Himachal Pradesh and Rajasthan) held additional charges.
2. Inadequate manpower in Block resource centres and cluster resource centres for monitoring and capacity building.

Children Out of Schools/Student Absenteeism

1. Universal enrolment is a difficult challenge due to seasonal migration, illiteracy, sibling care and economic backwardness.
2. Non-availability of multilingual schools, no uniform curriculum across states and non-availability of multilingual textbooks poses problems in achieving universal retention. School academic year is not in sync with migratory seasons.
3. Student absenteeism was high in Assam, Bihar and Uttar Pradesh due to seasonal migration and work at home. Parental negligence and lack of midday meals in schools also contributed to absenteeism.

Inadequate Funds/Untimely Release of Funds

1. Quarterly disbursements at sub block levels could lead to better utilization as second instalment was disbursed as late as January/March of the financial year.
2. No allocation of budgetary funds for karaikal district (Puducherry) separately.
3. Late receipt of funds in Assam, Haryana, Rajasthan and West Bengal. Monthly disbursements to Village/School education committees desirable.
4. Districts get funds under rigid heads, non-flexibility in deployment of resources.
5. Inadequate funds for schools in urban slum areas.

Community Ownership/Participation Weak

1. Though community initiatives are vital to strengthen implementation, responsibility lies entirely on headmaster of schools.
2. Training imparted for members of VECs not reflected in greater sense of ownership, transparency in usage of funds (display on notice board largely absent in schools) or maintenance of records. School management committees appear to be more effective.
3. Awareness of SSA interventions and PTAs are generally poor.

Weak linkages in Monitoring and Supervision

1. Composition of district level monitoring teams restricted to a few members including accountants, data entry operators. Most do not have representatives of DIET or NGOs. No records available at school level of visits by block or district teams.
2. No clarity on roles, responsibilities of BRCs/CRCs. Very few CRCs functioning from schools.
3. No nodal agency for implementation of SSA in urban areas. Each municipal corporation handles schools within

its jurisdiction, independent of the district authority. Town level committees lack commitment.

4. Involvement of NGOs limited to a few activities and at district or block level. No presence at village level.

9. RECOMMENDATIONS/SUGGESTIONS

A. To Reduce Dropouts/Out of School Children

1. Need to make upper primary-primary school ratio more favourable at village level and in urban slums by opening more upper primary schools or composite schools.
2. Pre-primary sections linked to primary schools more effective in reducing dropouts.
3. Reform schooling system with multilingual schools/ multi-grade textbooks.
4. Involvement of NGOs and CRCs to be sought for promoting awareness amongst parents of dropouts/out of school children.
5. Transport facilities to be provided to bring children from remote habitations to schools.
6. No detention policy to be followed by all states at primary levels.
7. District officials to devise academic calendar in sync with migratory seasons for improving retention rates amongst migratory students.
8. Migratory cards/seasonal hostels/resource persons to be appointed for mainstreaming out of school children.
9. NPEGEL schemes/vocational schools in Urban slums.
10. Free uniforms and financial incentives for children living in urban slums.

B. To Improve Teacher and Student Attendance

1. Introduction of Biometric systems of recording teacher attendance.

2. Non-teaching activities to be reduced, teachers not to supervise civil works, cattle surveys.
3. Midday meals to be provided in all schools in Bihar and Assam to improve student attendance. Schools in Puducherry provide breakfast to children which have improved retention.
4. Sports equipment need to be provided in schools.
5. Punishment to be avoided to discipline students.
6. Individualised education plans necessary for all differently-abled children. Incentives for attendance to be extended to these children.

C. To Improve the Quality of Education

1. Recruitment of teachers to fill vacancies, reduce high PTRs as well as different teachers for each subject at upper primary level.
2. A child friendly curriculum and system of assessment to move from examination based to continuous appraisal.
3. Improved pedagogic practices such as use of ABL and ALM methodologies.
4. Emphasis on writing skills rather than on rote learning. Workbooks to be provided to all children to make learning interesting.
5. Teachers to be consulted/opinion sought in curriculum construction.
6. Textbooks made available to all children in the beginning of the session irrespective of caste/gender.
7. Teacher training programmes to be redesigned for multi-grade teaching methods. Use of TLMs to be mandatory in teaching processes.
8. CRCs to be set up closer to the schools and catchment area for each CRC to be fixed. Academic guidance by CRC to include preparation of TLMs.

9. School libraries to be set up in all schools and reading habits to be encouraged.
10. Spending on quality interventions at district level to be improved.
11. VECs to be provided funds for appointment of para teachers to overcome teacher shortage.

D. To Improve School Environment

1. Separate toilet for Girls in all upper primary schools and ramps in all schools.
2. Drinking water to be provided in all schools.
3. Electricity to be provided in all schools to make effective use of computers.
4. Boundary walls/fencing in all schools to avoid straying of cattle, thefts of computers/fans etc.
5. Government-aided schools in rented buildings to be provided maintenance/repair grant to provide better infrastructure.
6. Appropriate funding for schools in urban slum areas.
7. Accreditation of schools based on school environment, inclusive education, extra curricular activities and quality of learning.

E. To Improve Monitoring/Supervision

1. School coordinators to be appointed in CRCs for monitoring teacher attendance and PTA/MTA meetings.
2. School management committees to have student representatives to inculcate leadership skills.
3. District level monitoring committees to have representatives from DIET, NGOs and subject experts. Monitoring of quality including school mapping to be made mandatory and report to be sent on quarterly basis to State project directors.

4. Display of receipt of funds on school notice boards to be made mandatory and VECs to be funded for appointment of cleaners/sweepers/security staff in schools.
5. Contingency/travel allowance at block level to be enhanced. Telephone facilities to be provided in BRCs and CRCs.
6. Regular monitoring at different levels and by different agencies can energise the community to accept more responsibility towards their schools. NGOs to be utilised for improving stakeholder participation.
7. Nodal agency for urban schools and separate plans formulated for urban slum schools.

Achievements of Sarva Shiksha Abhiyan (Up to 2015-16)

(1) Total enrolment in elementary schools has risen to 19.67 crore children. (2) Pupil Teacher Ratio (PTR) has improved to 25. (3) Number of Out of School children has come down to 60.64 lakh. (4) Average Annual Dropout rate at primary level has come down to 4.13% and average Annual Dropout rate at upper primary level is 4.03%. (5) The transition rate from primary to upper primary has gone up to 90.14%. (6) Gender Parity Index (GPI) has reached 0.93 for primary level and 0.95 at upper primary level. (7) Enrolment of SC children has gone up to 19.79% at elementary level. (8) Enrolment of ST children is 10.35% at elementary level. (9) Enrolment of Muslim children has grown up to 13.80% at elementary level. (10) 10,76,994 government school are operational in India whereas 1,62,237 primary schools and 78,903 upper primary schools have been opened during the period 2002-03 to 2015-16.

2

Foreign Policy

Foreign policy of the BJP has been inspired by the Hindu philosophy of universalism, liberalism, respect for the views of the other individuals and entities, and the concept of peaceful co-existence. The BJP, therefore, visualised the need for a peaceful international environment in which to pursue the goal of India's all-round development. It also realised that the rapidly shrinking world necessitated an extensive interaction with other countries and, therefore, prepared its plans for a pragmatic non-doctrinaire foreign policy.

Within the parameters of this broad vision, the BJP persuade on foreign policy rooted firmly in principles of national interest, national integrity and national security. A good policy, according to Kautilya, must achieve four things: to acquire what the nation does not have, to preserve what it has, to enhance what is preserved, and to use for the welfare of the people what is enhanced. Foreign policy, too, has to serve these ends. To achieve these objectives, the state needs power. As Kautilya says, "Power is the only means to ensure friendly relations with other nations." The BJP has been guided by this fundamental precept in its foreign policy. Ever since its formation in 1980, the Bharatiya Janata

Party has taken keen interest in foreign affairs and clearly expressed its views on foreign policy issues in numerous resolutions passed and the statements issued on various occasions. It clearly spelled out its foreign policy goals while it was in the opposition. And then went out to implement those policies when it formed its own Government along with coalition partners. The party was fortunate that one of its foremost leaders, Atal Bihari Vajpayee took special interest in foreign affairs as Foreign Minister in VP Singh government and later on as Prime Minister himself during 1998-2004. He, more than any other in the political arena, realised the importance of foreign policy in the overall development of the nation. Rapid scientific and technological developments were transforming the world into a global village and a large number of issues of national concern were acquiring a foreign policy dimension. Atalji gave expression to the party's views on national affairs in the numerous interventions he made in Parliament and in his addresses at different party functions from time to time.

The extent to which the BJP attached importance to the safeguarding of the national interest is reflected in several party resolutions over the years. The party reacted sharply to instances of the previous regime's tendency to overlook national interest in the pursuit of pet theories or doctrines. It has been the party's view that our national interest is best served by creating an environment of peace and harmony in our neighbourhood. But this can only be done on the basis of mutual benefit and cooperation. Right from the time of its inception, the party has emphasised the need for closer interaction with all our neighbouring countries and after coming into power, the BJP-led government made a special effort in this regard. Our concerns, however, go beyond our neighbourhood and our national interest requires a much broader range of interaction with major powers across the globe.

National security is another subject that has agitated the minds of the leaders of the party. A strong and prosperous India cannot be built without developing the capacity to defend the country against external threats. Our security concerns make it imperative that unless all countries agree to a time-bound programme of disarmament, India must have a minimum credible deterrent. That was the rationale for the series of nuclear tests in May 1998. The party manifestos of 1996 and 1998 had clearly stated the party's resolve to exercise the nuclear option and induct nuclear weapons into our security system. The BJP-led National Democratic Alliance government successfully met the diplomatic challenges in the aftermath of the nuclear tests.

BJP has always believed in the inherent strength and capability of India to emerge as a strong entity in the international arena. It visualises a multy-polar international scenario in which India must play a significant part. During the cold war period, the BJP supported the policy of genuine non-alignment but its ideological affinity with western democracies was quite apparent. The party also appreciated the need for cordial and mutually financial relationship with the Soviet Union. The party, however, expressed dismay over the unnecessarily pro-Soviet stand of the Congress Party.

Economic affairs have become an inseparable part of modern diplomacy and foreign policy formulation. BJP took note of this trend and developed its own views on economic issues. The party has shed some of its earlier conservatism and has extended support to the emerging new trends in a globalized world. The party has always advocated a strong economic dimension to our diplomacy and continues to lay special emphasis on economic interaction, especially in our neighbourhood, by participation in appropriate regional economic entities.

The BJP has been a consistent advocate of close contacts with the people origin settled abroad. Many of them have become citizens of other countries but practically all of them maintain some contacts with the mother country. It has taken the view that India should extend all possible assistance to them so that they remain in touch with their cultural roots. During the time that the party was in power, it made special efforts to involve the Indian Diaspora in close contacts with India. Besides the cultural connection, the political and economic cloud enjoyed by the Indian community in certain countries has created new linkages, which have been of considerable assistance to India.

Aware of the fact that foreign policy has now acquired a variety of new dimensions, the BJP has taken a very broad approach to foreign policy issues. An increasing number of issues from human rights and environmental issues, to gender questions and child labour, are rapidly acquiring an international character. The proper understanding of the foreign policy of a political party has become much more important today than was the case a few years ago.

BHARATIYA JANA SANGH PERIOD

The foreign policy orientation of the BJP has been influenced very largely by the policies of its earlier incarnation, the Bharatiya Jana Sangh (BJS). The BJS was established in 1951 by Dr Syama Prasad Mookerjee, an erstwhile member of the Union Cabinet, to provide an alternative to some of Jawaharlal Nehru's views with which he strongly disagreed. There is a widespread but erroneous impression that he formed the new political party to promote the sectarian and community interests of the Hindus and to protest against the extreme indulgence shown to the Muslim population by the Congress Party. There may be some truth in the impression that the Hindus reacted strongly to the over-protective policies of the Congress towards the Muslim community but that was certainly not the only reason for Dr SP Mookerjee to promote a new party. He strongly disagreed with Jawaharlal Nehru on the following foreign policy related issues:

1. Relations with Pakistan and handling of the Kashmir issue.
2. Socialist policies and relations with the communist countries.
3. Status of Tibet and policy towards China.
4. Handling of matters relating to the Hindu minority in the East Pakistan.

The Bharatiya Jana Sangh was a very small but significant political entity in the 1950s. But its voice was heard because of the stringent criticism it made of some of the policies pursued by Prime Minister Jawaharlal Nehru and because of widespread impression that the party represented the views of a large number of people. Even as small a party in the 1950s, the Bharatiya Jana Sangh developed its own views on foreign policy issues. The party expressed firmly its views on important issues of that period through the statements made by its leaders and resolutions passed at the Working Committee of the party. One of the major questions taken up by the Bharatiya Jana Sangh in the 1950s was the policy pursued by the Government of India towards Pakistan. It strongly criticised the manner in which matters relating to the State of Jammu and Kashmir were being handled. Bharatiya Jana Sangh launched a campaign for the abrogation of Article 370 of the Constitution and wanted Jammu and Kashmir to have the same status as that of any other state in India. It was highly critical of the Government of India's decision to take the issues to the United Nations Security Council. In a Resolution passed by the Working Committee of the party on November 24, 1957 it stated that:

> The recent developments at the UN Security Council regarding Jammu-Kashmir have demonstrated once

again that the UNO has got itself involved in power politics so much that it would be futile to expect justice and fair-play from it.

The Central Working Committee, therefore, feels that no useful purpose can be served by keeping the question open for discussion at the UNO. It urges upon the Government to withdraw the Kashmir issue from there and desist from wasting any more money, time, and energy in trying to convince those who are determined not too be convinced. It further urges upon the Government to take all immediate effective steps to recover possession of the Kashmir territory now aggressively occupied by Pakistan. Kashmir is essentially a domestic issue and must be tackled as such with the cooperation of all-sections of the Indian opinion who are united on this vital national issue.

The Committee further feels that time has now come when the temporary distinction between Jammu-Kashmir state and the rest of India as envisaged in Article 370 of the Indian Constitution be removed once for all and the Jammu-Kashmir state be brought in line with the rest of India in all respects. This, the Committee is convinced, is essential to bring about the emotional integration of the people of that state with their co-citizens of the rest of India and checkmate the designs of separatist and anti-national elements within and outside Kashmir, who have been exploiting these distinctions to the detriment of the wider interests of India including Kashmir.

Bharatiya Jana Sangh strongly believed that in order to establish India's position in Kashmir and to guard against separatism, it was essential to take steps for complete emotional, cultural and administrative oneness between Kashmir and the rest of India. This could not be achieved. If distinctiveness was manifested through separate Constitution, separate Flag, separate President, separate Election Commission and separate Law on citizenship for the State of Jammu and Kashmir. The party stressed that Jammu and Kashmir must be made an integral part of India.

Relation with China

On the question of relations with China, the Bharatiya Jana Sangh, while expressing a desire for good relations with the big neighbour, expressed utter dismay at the treatment meted out by the Chinese to the Tibetans. It maintained that communist China took over Tibet by sheer force of arms and imposed an agreement upon the Tibetan Government of his holiness, the Dalai Lama under duress, effecting the subjugation of Tibet and conceding here only a semblance of autonomy.

Tibet

In the Resolution passed on July 8, 1959 in its governing council the party stated that for the tragedy that had overtaken Tibet, the Government of India could not escape her share of responsibility. In fact with the weak-kneed and short-sighted policy followed by the Nehru Government had encouraged China in her aggressive policy in Tibet. It felt that India should take immediate and an effective steps to bring an end to the Chinese aggression in Tibet and for the withdrawal of her armies of occupation from Tibet. Bharatiya Jana Sangh accordingly proposed that:

1. India herself should move the United Nations to take up Tibet's case. In fact, the Tibet issue had been raised in the UN when China overran her about 9 years ago, but it was at India's request and insistence that the matter was shelved and practically dropped. Now that China has gone back upon her pledge of respecting Tibet's autonomy, and her words have proved undependable, India owes it to herself to raise the Tibetan issue at the UN.

2. India should approach the Free Nations of Asia (outside Communist orbit) on the issue of China's aggression in Tibet so that they might make common cause in support of Tibet's independence. Already, China's aggression in Tibet has caused apprehension in Eastern Asia; and people there are beginning to feel that the occupation of Tibet is only the first step of China's ambition towards imperialistic expansion. The banding together of the Free Nations of Asia in an attitude of protest may produce some sober effect even on the ruthless and ambitious rulers of Communist China who may yet pause in their predatory activities. Even at this late stage, China may care something for Asian opinion.
3. In the meantime, full facilities should be given to His Holiness the Dalai Lama to function in India on the political plane as the Government of Tibet. If Tibetan independence is to be striven for and secured, it will not do simply to grant him asylum and to keep him in a sort of enforced retirement free to function only in his spiritual capacity, but he should be allowed in India to work for the cause of Tibet's independence.

Further, apart from all other considerations, from the point of view of India's own safety and security alone, it is essential that China must clear out of Tibet, and that Tibet should become an Independent State. India should, therefore, direct all her efforts towards securing Tibet's Independence.

In a later Resolution passed by the party after the Chinese invasion on October 1962, the party called upon the Government to extend help to the Tibetan freedom fighters. It was of the view that the Indian Government must recognise the sovereignty of Tibet and the Dalai Lama's emigre Government.

In this Resolution passed on October 31,1962, at the Central Working Committee of the party, the Bharatiya

Jana Sangh viewed with grave concern the situation created by the Chinese invasion in Ladakh and NEFA. It accused the Government of being totally unprepared in terms of both the strength in numbers and the quality and the quantity of equipment. It charged that this had been due to the wrong appraisal of China's intentions, preparations and former intrusions into Indian territory.

Support to Democracies

The Bharatiya Jana Sangh did not approve of the policy of the Government of India to befriend communist countries at the cost of our relationship with other nations. It noted with grave concern the assertion of the totalitarian trends in Russia and its growing stronghold on the satellite countries of Eastern Europe. The party expressed itself in favour of true democracy based on freedom of individual and equality of opportunity to all, irrespective of caste, creed or colour and the right of all people to decide freely about the form of the Government that they would like to have. In a Resolution passed on April 5, 1963, the party stated that -

> Bharatiya Jana Sangh is a firm-believer in democracy and wants it to succeed so that the world might be saved from the rising tide of totalitarianism and demands that while professing to pursue an independent policy of non-alignment, Government of India should not create the impression—even by implication—that they are inclined towards one camp or the other. Such an impression if it is allowed to grow is neither in the enlightened self-interests of India nor of peace and democracy in the world as a whole.

EVOLUTION OF JANA SANGH

The Jana Sangh party was the formative stage of the Bharatiya Janata Party's policy. During the four years since

Independence before Jana Sangh came into the picture, the ruling party had already outlined the broad contours of the country's foreign policy. Prime Minister Nehru's forays into international diplomacy had earned him accolades from his countrymen but while appreciating his contribution to the development of the India's foreign policy, the Jana Sangh did not fail to notice some chinks in his armour. It was pointed out that Nehru had failed the country in his policies towards Pakistan and China, that he had been taken for a ride on the issues of Kashmir and Tibet, that his fascination for socialism was pushing him towards close relations with the communist countries, at the cost of India's friendship with western democratic countries, and that he failed to recognise that morality and fair play had very little relevance in international relations.

In his second speech in the Lok Sabha, Atal Bihari Vajpayee outlined the views of his party on various foreign issues. He charged that Nehru's policies had failed to win friends for India. He felt that the Prime Minister was so occupied with international issues in other countries that he had forgotten to safeguard the interests of this country on matters that were important from India's point of view. He remarked,

> We help some countries and try to solve their problems, but even those countries are not extending their firm support to the Indian cause over the Kashmir issue.

Emphasising the need for pursuing pragmatic policies in the pursuit of national interest, he strongly advocated a change in India's approach. His views on this subject as stated in his above mentioned speech are quoted ahead:

> In this respect there is another aspect that has become clear. It is that international politics does not work on the basis of morality. There is no place for selfless dedicated work. We may burn our hands while performing *havan* and also create now policy needs to accord with the

> realities of international politics but this is to be done carefully in view of the current situation, when we badly need the cooperation, help and support of all countries. As regards Indian policy of not aligning with any bloc, we fully support it. As far as my party, Bharatiya Jana Sangh is concerned, we agree with the policy that we should not join either the American or the Russian block, as doing so is in the interest of the country.

During the 1960s, the Government of India's policies with regard to China and Pakistan came under the severe attack from the Jana Sangh. Prime Minister Nehru himself admitted failure of his China policy and it gave an opportunity to the Jana Sangh to demand re-orientation of foreign policy. It also demanded that India should not recognise China's sovereignty over Tibet and the government should accord recognition to the Dalai Lama as a head of Tibet emigre Government. The relevant extract from the Resolution passed on December 30, 1962 quoted below:

> The failure of the Government of India's China Policy is a pointed manifestation of the fact that in the realm of international affairs, our policies have lacked a substratum of realism and have ignored the need to safeguard the enlightened self-interests of the nation. Despite our advocacy of non-alignment, in practice, our policies have tended to lean towards the Soviet bloc. Besides, we have been indifferent to the imperative concomitant of this policy of non-alignment, namely, the building up of adequate military strength. A re-evaluation and re-orientation of our foreign policy with a view to ensuring effectively the country's security has, therefore, become essential.
>
> Our policy of not aligning ourselves with either of the power blocs has in no way impeded procurement of military assistance from friendly countries nor does it

> prevent us from endeavouring to build up an association of peace-loving countries in order to contain Chinese expansionism.
>
> It is necessary for India to strengthen its relations with the countries who have helped us against communist China and at the same time to strive to secure the support of other countries too. It should be our endeavour also to see that nations which for any reason are not prepared to support us do not line up with China either. Let us refuse to recognise China's authority over countries it has forcibly enchained and extent all support we can, to help them regain their independence. Dalai Lama should be recognised as Head of Tibet's emigre Government.
>
> The Jana Sangh welcomes improvement in Indo-Nepalese relations that has lately been evident. To enhance this cordial turn we ought to make a conscious attempt to eliminate any misunderstandings that may still be subsisting between the two.

India's conflict with China resulting in a humiliating defeat encouraged Pakistan to adopt a stringent approach towards India, the signing of the Sino-Pak agreement under which Pakistan ceded a portion of the Pak-Occupied Kashmir to China was the beginning of a long-term bilateral friendship. Pakistan began to put pressure on India, especially through the United States to resolve the issue of Kashmir. Pakistan thought that this was an excellent opportunity to compel India to handover the valley to Pakistan. When the Government of India entered into negotiations with Pakistan, the Bharatiya Jana Sangh felt that the Government of India's policy towards Pakistan, smacked of imbecility. The resolution passed on December 30, 1963 had the following to say on the subject:

> It has been the considered view of the Bharatiya Jana Sangh that Pakistan by its very genesis and nature is

destined to treat India as its enemy No. 1, so long as it exists. Hostility to India and Hindus is the only prop, which keeps going this artificial state of two parts separated by a thousand miles of Indian territory. Its continual adventures against India, the continuous anti-India and anti-Hindu population, which has been deprived of even its basic human rights and which is being steadily decimated through physical extermination, their conversion and forcible expulsion from Pakistan and encouragement of Naga hostiles are manifestations of a set policy of keeping at the highest pitch the anti-India and anti-Hindu frenzy in Pakistan at all times. It would be wrong to hope that Pakistan would change its attitude if Kashmir question was solved, to its satisfaction because the so-called Kashmir problem is just a facet of Pakistani policies. Pakistan will always whip-up some problems or the other even if the existing ones are settled to her entire satisfaction to keep that frenzy on.

Jana Sangh does not consider it a matter to gloat over, that this analysis of Jana Sangh about Pakistan's attitude towards India has been vindicated by the actual course of events, particularly since the Chinese invasion of India, and is now being gradually accepted at all hands.

Jawaharlal Nehru's policies on the Kashmir issue were to remain the subject of very strong criticism from the Bharatiya Jana Sangh. In Resolution passed specifically on the Kashmir problem on May 25, 1964, just before the death of Prime Minister Nehru, that party stated that Kashmir had been an integral part of India historically, geographically, culturally all three aegis. The formal accession state of India on October 1947 by the Ruler gave legal and constitutional sanction of that historical fact. It accused Jawaharlal Nehru of committing several blunders in the handling of the Kashmir issue. In this regard, the Resolution stated:

But unfortunately, Nehru who has been handling Kashmir question on behalf of Government of India and treating it almost as a personal affair, began his bungling from that very moment. He readily fell into the trap of Jinnah, who finding his plan of military conquest of the state and presenting the world with the fait accompli, foiled by the accession of the state of India and arrival of Indian army on the scene, decided to politicalise the issue. The unilateral and illegal offer of plebiscite and its continuous repetition, appeal to the UNO, failure to explicitly name Pakistan as aggressor in the original complaint to UNO, failure to send right men to plead India's case there, ordering of cease fire when the Indian troops were advancing on all fronts, failure to settle Hindu refuges uprooted by Pakistani invaders, in Kashmir in spite of their repeated requests, failure to exercise effective check on Kashmir administration and incorporation of temporary Article 370 in the Indian Constitution to appease Sheikh Abdullah's ambitions were series of the early blunders committed by the Nehru Government in regard to Kashmir.

TASHKENT DECLARATION

The Bharatiya Jana Sangh felt that the Tashkent Declaration that emerged from the Indo-Pak Summit hosted by the Soviet Union had caused deep disappointment in the country. It was of the opinion that the Declaration was no assurance of stable or real peace between India and Pakistan. It was pointed out that Pakistan had refused to agree to any categorical no-war pact. Pakistan's argument for the rejection of the no-war proposal clearly showed that it was in no way prepared to renounce use of force until the Kashmir problem was settled. The BJS went on to warn that the Government of India would be indulging in self-delusion if it thought that the Tashkent Declaration meant the end of Pakistan's aggressive intentions.

In a Resolution passed on July 2, 1966, the BJS Central Working Committee demanded, among other things, that defence preparations in the country must be stepped up and immediate steps must be taken to increase the strength of the defence forces and develop an independent nuclear deterrent. It also demanded that India must make it clear to Pakistan and the world at large once for all that Kashmir was not negotiable.

Bangladesh War and Simla Agreement

The Bharatiya Jana Sangh had consistently raised the question of treatment of minorities in East Bengal and particularly the treatment meted out to the Hindus living in the East Pakistan. When the Bangladesh war began, the party, extended full support to the aspirations of the Bangladeshis in East Bengal. It also lent full support to the liberation movement. The Bharatiya Jana Sangh accorded a qualified welcome to the Indo-Soviet Treaty of Peace, Friendship and Cooperation. It hoped that the treaty will help to counter the continued American arming of Pakistan and the Chinese intervention in Indo-Pak affairs. The party, however, was not prepared to extend uncritical support to the treaty and wished to judge it only by the contribution it would make to the freedom of Bangladesh. It also expressed its firm conviction that if the treaty was to work to the equal advantage of both countries, India must grow in strength to become an independent power centre. It also emphasised that for this purpose, the development of a nuclear capability is of the utmost importance.

The Simla Agreement signed in June 1972 was described by the Bharatiya Jana Sangh as a complete sell-out. The party was of the view that India had given into all demands of Pakistan without getting anything in return.

It maintained that India had lost the opportunity to settle once for all the question of Kashmir. The party demanded the immediate scrapping of the Simla Agreement.

Arab-Israeli Conflict

At the time of the Arab-Israeli war in 1967, the Bharatiya Jana Sangh disapproved of the partisan policy pursued by the Government of India in regard to the West Asia conflict. It believed that India should have exerted its influence to check any eruption of hostilities between the Arabs and the Israelis and that after the war had broken out, India should have tried to restore peace. Instead, Government of India had extended outright support to the Arabs. In a Resolution passed on June 30, 1967 the Central Working Committee of the party said,

> Bharatiya Jana Sangh demands that the Government of India must revise its West Asia policy with a view to winning the friendship of both Arabs and Israelis and creating stable peace in the region. In this context the Jana Sangh wishes to reiterate its demand that the Government of India must take steps to establish full-fledged diplomatic relations with Israel.

In a resolution passed by the party in November 1973 after the 1973 West Asia crises, the party criticised the Government of India for its inept handling of the West Asia situation. It says,

> By taking sides in a most blatant manner, it has ruled itself out of any mediatory role in an area crucial to our vital national interests. By going more Arabian than Arabs, New Delhi has neither served national interest nor promoted the cause of peace. In this connection it is revealing that New Delhi's over enthusiastic support to the Arabs notwithstanding, Saudi Arabia has decided to cut its oil supplies to India. It is obvious that New Delhi's West Asia policy is conditioned by the ruling party's obsession with the communal vote.

The party called upon the Government of India to overhaul its West Asia policy. It suggested to the Government that it should work for friendship with both sides and, as a first step in that direction, normalise its relations with Israel by establishing diplomatic ties.

Dissolution of Bharatiya Jana Sangh

A state of Emergency was declared by the Government of India in June 1975. Most of the prominent leaders of the Bharatiya Jana Sangh, along with many of other political parties were arrested for a period of 19 months. No political activity by Opposition parties was permitted during this time. In March 1977, when the General Elections were held, several opposition parties combined to form the Janata Party and won a landslide victory. The Bharatiya Jana Sangh had also merged with the new party and nearly 100 of its members were elected to the Lok Sabha. The party's leaders, Atal Bihari Vajpayee was given the post of Minister of Foreign Affairs by Prime Minister Morarji Desai. During the rather short tenure of 2½ years, the Janata Party introduced some subtle changes in the foreign policy orientation of the country. The policy became more pragmatic and non-doctrinaire. The policy of good relations with the Soviet Union was maintained but without the euphoria of the preceding years. Attempts were made to establish a new equation with the United States and West European countries. The External Affairs Minister, Atal Bihari Vajpayee paid special attention to the development of close relations with all neighbouring countries. It is now recognised that the relations between India and Pakistan improved dramatically during the time when Vajpayee was guiding the foreign policy of the country.

Janata Party experiment was rather short lived and it split into its diverse constituents in the middle of 1979. The members of the erstwhile Bharatiya Jana Sangh decided to establish a new party and it was named the Bharatiya Janata Party. It came into being on April 6, 1980.

THE 1980s

The decade of 1980s was a period of re-grouping and reconstitution for the Bharatiya Janata Party. It had a comparatively much lower representation in Parliament as compared with the preceding years but its numbers in the Lok Sabha rose dramatically from a mere two in 1984 to more than 100 in 1989. It was necessary and it indeed quite logical for the party to concentrate on domestic issues during the early years of newly established organisation. The party, however, did not delink itself from the ideology of its previous incarnation, namely, the Bharatiya Jana Sangh. On foreign policy issues, therefore, there was a fair amount of continuity. The party expressed its views frequently on a wide verity of developments related to foreign affairs.

Some of the prominent events that took place soon after the formation of BJP were the Soviet intervention in Afghanistan, turmoil in the non-aligned movement, the Iran-Iraq war and the ethnic conflict in Sri Lanka. On all these issues, the Bharatiya Janata Party expressed its views through the party resolutions, comments by its spokesmen, speeches of the party president and other senior leaders and during the debates in Parliament.

Afghanistan

The BJP viewed the developments in Afghanistan as a setback to global detente and as an accentuation of superpower rivalry. It considered the Soviet military intervention, which later resulted in virtual occupation as a violation of the UN Charter and as a blow to the aspirations and the ideals of the non-aligned movement. It was, in the party's view, a contravention of all canons of international law and behaviour. The party criticised strongly the attitude adopted by the Indira Gandhi government on this issue. The Indian government's support to the Soviet action had resulted in the lowering of India's prestige in the eyes of the world and in isolating us from our neighbours. In a Resolution adopted on September 5, 1980, the BJP recalled,

> The Janata government had succeeded in deepening and strengthening the bonds of Indo-Soviet friendship. A programme of long-range cooperation in the economic field was drawn up in those days. Indo-Soviet friendship was strengthened on the basis of equality and mutual cooperation. The Bharatiya Janata Party would like to see further strengthening of Indo-Soviet ties.
>
> The party, however, does not believe that the bonds of Indo-Soviet friendship are so fragile as to be shattered merely by calling a spade a spade. The continued presence of Soviet armed forces in Afghanistan is totally unjustified and India's determination to pursue an independent foreign policy demands that words should not be minced in this matter.

In a later Resolution BJP attributed the Soviet occupation to the questionable concept of spheres of influence. It thoroughly criticised the concept and expressed the view that it had vital short-term and long-term consequences for India as a nation. The BJP called upon the Government of India to take the lead for a regional, non-aligned initiative to ensure that Afghanistan regained its independent status. It also expressed its regret that the non-aligned movement had failed to come up with any new initiative for a resolution against the continued presence of Soviet troops in Afghanistan.

Non-Alignment

During the tenure of the Janata government when Atal Bihari Vajpayee was the Foreign Minister, the Janata government had asserted that it would pursue a policy of genuine non-alignment without tilting towards any superpower. The Bharatiya Janata Party believed that this policy had brought dividends for India and that our image abroad had brightened. The party regretted that within a year of the new government taking over, distortions once again crept into matters concerning our foreign policy. The party believed that India should not only remain non-aligned, but should also appear to be so. The BJP also criticised attempts by Mrs Gandhi and her companions to drag India's relations with other countries into the domestic election controversies. These attempts had given a serious setback to the process of evolving a consensus-based foreign policy. The party strongly believed that it was only by sincerely adhering to the principle of genuine non-alignment that the country would be able to contribute its mite towards freedom peace and progress in the world. In a Resolution adopted on April 23, 1981, the party noted with concern that –

> The erosion that is being permitted by the present government to the original principle of non-alignment. India's voice no longer commands the respect that it once did in the comity of nations. Ambivalence, not independent views, has come to represent us. Our stand on Afghanistan and recognition of Kampuchea has served neither our national interests nor any principle. We have in the process alienated large and significant sections of the non-aligned. The BJP is appreciative of the commonality of ties with USSR. We would work towards further strengthening of these ties on the basis of equality and mutual benefit. We are, however, constrained to observe that never before in the past 34 years of our independent history has an Indian Prime Minister taken on the role of a spokesman and interpreter of the strategic perceptions of a superpower.

A few years later, the then President of BJP, LK Advani pointed out that it was the Janata Party government that correctly pursued the non-aligned policy. He made the following comments at the National Council meeting on May 9, 1986:

In Mrs Gandhi's days, India's friendship with the USSR was always viewed with suspicion by the Western blocks. Our declarations of non-alignment were distrusted. The Janata government during its brief tenure tried to dispel this distrust. And it succeeded remarkably. While our warm and close ties with the Soviet Union continued as ever, a very good rapport was built up also with the West. India's non-alignment acquired credibility. Unfortunately, in recent months while in the Western block the earlier distrust has returned, particularly with the Libyan incident, there is some cooling off even in the Soviet block. When recently Secretary General Gorbachov presented his report to the CPSU, he conspicuously omitted even a reference to India. This is a pointer, whose significance cannot be missed.

IRAN-IRAQ CONFLICT AND PALESTINIAN PROBLEM

The BJP viewed the unfortunate continuation of Iran-Iraq war as being inimical to larger Arab interests and as likely to divert world attention from the crucial aspect of a final settlement of the Palestinian question. The party believed that the gulf countries had become the core of multiple tensions heightened by a clash of superpower interests. It called upon the non-aligned movement to play a crucial role in assisting towards a resolution of the problems of the region.

On the Palestinian question, the party held the view that the solution to the problem can be found through UN Resolutions on the subject. It also believe that the right of Palestinians to homeland cannot be denied. Israel had the right to exist but not as an expanding regional power, with freedom to define its own concept of secure frontiers.

Sri Lanka

The Bharatiya Janata Party was gravely concerned about the ethnic conflict in Sri Lanka. In the opinion of the party, the government and the people of India could not but be concerned with the unfortunate developments in so close a neighbouring country. In a Resolution adopted at the National Executive meeting of the party on May 6, 1986, the party stated the following:

> The sorry condition of a large number of Tamilian citizens and residents of Sri Lanka, the hostile discrimination persistently practised against them in various matters such as education, employment under the state, economic opportunities and land settlement, and their ruthless suppression by the instrumentalities of the state inevitably evoke sympathy of the people of India and cause ripples of resentment and anger. The Government of India cannot forever remain insensitive to the acute social tensions that are building up inside India. Apart from the historic ties of ethnic origin and affinity and blood relationships that fully justify Indian involvement in the destiny of Tamil Lankans, no civilised government can turn a Nelson's eye to widespread, persistent and organised violation of basic human rights of fellow human beings in any part of the world more so in a country only a few miles away from ourselves.

The BJP believed that the conflict in Sri Lanka was a multidimensional one. It involved a sharing of political power between the majority Singhala and the minority Tamils, equal economic opportunities for both the communities and peaceful co-existence among different religious communities. The Bharatiya Janata Party at the same time warned the Tamilian groups that they should not take recourse to violence and not do anything to affect the integrity of Sri Lanka. In its above-mentioned resolution, the party stated:

> The Bharatiya Janata Party has also a caution to utter to the Tamilian groups involved in the conflict. If they

practice violence and murder on one another, any justification for protest against state violence disappears. Internecine quarrels and squabbles must inevitably hurt their cause. They must, therefore, close their ranks and speak with one voice to carry weight and credibility.

The Bharatiya Janata Party while being aware of the provocation for violence cannot condone or approve of its use. Nor can the Bharatiya Janata Party encourage a movement to dismember a sovereign state, which a member of the United Nations and the Commonwealth. The Bharatiya Janata Party, while striving to secure complete justice for the Tamilians, has inevitable limitations, which, as a responsible political party in a responsible country, it cannot overlook or breach.

South Asian Cooperation

The BJP has always been of the view that the countries of South Asia must engage in continues economic cooperation. The party felt that deteriorating economic conditions in the world were threatening political stability of developing countries and the only way out was cooperation with each other. It urged the Government of India to make the beginning towards economic recovery of the countries of the region by working for South Asian Region Cooperation for trade and commerce. The party believed that this effort could eventually lead to South Asian common market. It may be noted that BJP was one of the earliest and a strong supporter of the idea of South Asian Regional Cooperation.

BJP EMERGES AS A STRONG FORCE

During the second-half of the '80s and early '90s, there was considerable turmoil in the international arena. The Bharatiya Janata Party took a position on a variety of issues ranging from the end of the Cold War and UN reforms to the nearer home issues of Pakistani nuclear ambitions, cross-border terrorism and infiltration of Bangladeshis into India. The party also questioned the manner in which the foreign policy of the Government of India was being conducted by the Congress Party government. It strongly criticised the *ad hoc* manner in which the foreign policy was being executed. In a scathing criticism of the Government, the then President of the party, LK Advani stated at the National Executive meeting of the party in 1988:

> A principal plank to Rajiv Gandhi's early pronouncements on foreign policy was the establishment of a more stable relationship with our neighbouring countries. Now, three years into his unhappy premiership, one finds that never since independence have our relations with our neighbours been as strained, and as sour, as they are today. Starting from a personalised foreign policy of foreign jaunts in which, in the first 28 months of his premiership, Rajiv Gandhi engaged in 'Vishwa Darshan' by jetting, at enormous expense, to 35 countries, our country has by now been reduced to a status of almost regional inconsequence.
>
> Our bilateral relations are currently strained with Pakistan, the People's Republic of China, Bangladesh and Sri Lanka. The Socialist Republic of Burma has rejected our amateurish attempts at inviting them into the non-aligned fold. Face to face with prospects of Soviet withdrawal from Afghanistan, we search on telephone for an Afghanistan policy, and by an ill-thought-out initiative with President Zia. Never since the days of the Islamic Summit of Rabbat, in the sixties, has the nation suffered as humiliating a diplomatic rebuff as this juvenile telephone diplomacy of Rajiv Gandhi.
>
> This government sadly lacks a proper conceptual framework of foreign policy. What is more worrisome is that it totally fails on the front of execution of policy as well. Our foreign policy has become episodic and ad hoc. We combat apartheid by flamboyant ministerial

> statements in Parliament, while on the ground, the obscenity of racial discrimination proliferates. We play tennis with Israel one day, and do not one another, and call it policy, while China occupies our soil we talk only of improving relations, but not of freeing our territory of foreign occupation. While President Ershad announces his decision to convert Bangladesh into an Islamic Republic, we sit silently unconcerned about the fate of 15 million Hindus there; our only response is to cancel a cricket tour. In the context of the West Asian imbroglio and persecution of Palestinians, Rajiv Gandhi demonstrates irrelevance in South East Asia, particularly Kampuchea, inconsequence.
>
> As if to cover up all these monumental failures, recourse is then taken to festivals, in the USA, UK, Sweden, France, USSR and now in Japan, all in the name of cultural diplomacy!

At the same meeting Advani had also some comments on the irresponsible manner in which the government was responding to the mounting evidence of Pakistan's nuclear weapons programme. In his view, the government had failed to adopt a strong policy on the need for developing nuclear weapons. This, he believed, was a very significant failure of the Rajiv government.

End of the Cold War

With the Bharatiya Janata Party welcomed the end of the Cold War and the process of detente among major power, which replaced the hostile and ideologically competitive ideological relations with the spirit of cooperation and argument on various international and regional problems. The party congratulated the President of United States and the President of the Soviet Union for their wisdom and statesmanship on ending the Cold War and beginning the process of nuclear disarmament, which would diminish the threat of nuclear holocaust. The party welcomed the consequent end of communalism and advent of democracy in the Soviet Union. The party also recognised that the changed international situation was characterised by the emergence of one super alliance, the Euro-American Alliance, which also included the Soviet Union or Russia among its partners. It was also realised that the changed environment had brought new challenges before India and that the Government of India must take immediate steps in the fields of defence and foreign affairs to protect its vital interests.

The BJP appreciated the need for a review of India's foreign policy options in view of the rapid changes in the international scenario. The failure of the government to face the realities there committed upon by the party President, Murli Manohar Joshi at the meeting of the National Executive on April 6, 1990. He said,

> The Congress(I) Government, has also failed to appreciate the fast changing international scene. Its responses to the happenings in Eastern Europe and Russia have demonstrated the perfunctory attitude to international affairs. There is an urgent need to redefine India's foreign policy particularly when the arms race and cold war politics have lost their relevance. The recent cut in nuclear weapons is a welcome step but the BJP would like to have a fresh assessment of its security environment. Relations with neighbours should be constantly reviewed with a view to settling outstanding disputes. It is high time that the party should demand full diplomatic relations with Israel. In the new emerging international scene it would be the strength of a country's economy, which would determine its place in the comity of nations, and, therefore, it is imperative to take urgently measures for strengthening the economy of our country.

There were lots of expectations from the changes emerging after the Cold War. But the new era did not really bring about any significant changes. It was hoped that the end of the Cold War would usher in an era of peace, cooperation and all-round development of friendly relations among the nations of the world. This hope was belied and there was still conflict and tension in many parts of the world. The Bharatiya Janata Party expressed the view that the attempt to impose a new world order based on military and economic strength had vitiated in the international atmosphere. The political and economic dominations by some affluent countries was reminiscent of the colonial and imperialist era prevalent before Second World War.

One of the negative developments soon after the disintegration of the Soviet Union was the eruption of the Gulf War. It was widely seen as America's war for exploitation of energy resources of the Gulf region. The BJP took serious note of this development and called for protection of the country's economic interests by suitable adjustment of its foreign policy. Quoted below are the views of the President of the Bharatiya Janata Party at the National Council meeting held on February 1, 1991:

> The Gulf war will have a worldwide impact. The biggest of questions it has raised is, who will control oil? This is the latest example of the struggle for control over sources of energy. In the new international politics, economic diplomacy will acquire as much importance as political and strategic diplomacy. India must pay serious attention to its economic interests. It is the opinion of Bharatiya Janata Party that along with good relations with neighbouring countries protection of the country's economic interests should form an integral part of our foreign policy.

UN Reforms

The Bharatiya Janata Party had often commented upon the need of reforms in the UN system. It felt that the United Nations in its current form could not be the instrument to bring about a just order in the world. It emphasised the imperative need to reform the UN so as to democratise the world body in order to make it an effective instrument to bring about a new international order based on equality of nations. In its manifesto before the General Elections in 1996, the party stated, "The BJP will launch a vigorous campaign for a permanent membership for India in the UN Security Council." During the time that party came in power it did indeed campaign vigorously but unsuccessfully to secure for India a permanent place in the UN Security Council. The efforts are still continuing and, hopefully, India will get it well-deserved position in the UN system.

DECADE OF 1990s

The disintegration of the Soviet Union, the end of the Cold War and the emergence of the variously defined New World Order brought about an entirely new international scenario. The non-aligned movement lost quite a bit of its shine and some new ideas began to emerge. The role of the United Nations and the concept of national sovereignty were questioned. Many erstwhile national issues began to acquire an international character. Environmental issues, human rights questions, gender equality, labour-related matters, etc. (The list is actually quite long) acquired an international dimension. The BJP took note of all these developments and re-fashioned its views accordingly.

It was around this time that the Foreign Affairs Cell of the party was reconstituted and strengthened with the induction a number of retired Ambassadors. It was headed by a very distinguished diplomat, Brajesh Misra. A Defence Cell was also established with two outstanding officers of the Indian Army, Lt Gen KP Candeth and Lt Gen FRJ Jacob joining this cell. The Foreign Affairs and Defence Cells worked in tandem and under the guidance of Atal Bihari Vajpayee and LK Advani formulated the party's views on foreign affairs and national security related issues.

Beginning with the manifesto for the 1991 General Elections, the BJP began the process of evolving policies which it was to implement in some form or the other during the six years that the party was in power from 1998 onwards. The manifestos identified national interest, national integrity and national security as the principal elements of BJP's foreign policy goals.

The party noted that with the sudden disappearance of a bipolar divide of 45 years, the USSR and the US were no longer adversaries but partners. The curtains had finally been drawn over the Cold War that had dominated the world for most of the 20th century. International equations were changing fast. In the post-Cold War period, neither the USA needed Third World countries to counter communism nor did the USSR have any use any more for its so-called natural allies in the developing world. As a result, the non-align movement, which was created against the backdrop of the bipolar world, had lost its relevance.

The party came to the conclusion that the new situation was a challenging one and at the same time with several fresh opportunities for a larger Indian's role in global affairs. But only economically healthy, militarily strong and progressive India could carve out a niche for itself. As long as India went around with a begging bowl around the world, her voice in the international affairs will not be heard with respect. The party, therefore, concluded that Indian must be militarily strong and economically powerful to assert itself. To this end, the party proposed a number of steps to strengthen India's position in the international arena. These included the following:

1. Work for a stronger South Asian Association for Regional Cooperation in view of the old bipolar world giving place to all a unipolar world.
2. Promote the idea of a Common Market of all SAARC states.

3. Develop friendly and cordial relations with the countries of South-East Asia, with whom we have ancient cultural bonds.
4. Stand by persons of Indian origin abroad in defence of their legitimate rights.
5. Give dual citizenship to Indian citizens abroad.
6. Strive to strengthen the United Nations in view of the fact that in the changed situation the world powers are more inclined to work through the UN. Strive to make India an autonomous power in the world with a permanent seat in the UN Security Council.

It must be noted that in the proposed steps numerated above, there were some which were put forward for the first time and later became an important part of the Government of India's policies like the Look East Policy, closer contacts with the Indian Diaspora abroad and the idea of seeking a permanent seat in the UN Security Council.

ISLAMIC CONFERENCE

The BJP has always viewed with utmost concern the binding together of countries on the basis of religion:

> It is deplorable that the Organisation of Islamic Conference takes its political decisions on the basis of religion. Its resolutions on the Kashmir issue are an example of decisions dictated by religious sentiments. This is a tendency, which promotes disharmony in international relations, and the party believes that this needs to be discouraged. The OIC has also been used by Pakistan not only to get resolutions passed on Kashmir, but also in several other ways to damage India's interests in the international arena by propagating its anti-Indian views in the deliberations of the OIC.

Nuclear Threat from Pakistan and India's Nuclear Option

The BJP had often warned the Government of India of the emerging nuclear threat from Pakistan and it had also clearly expressed its viewed that India must exercise it nuclear option. The continued inaction of the Government of India prompted the party to issue a strongly worded statement at its National Council meeting on June 2, 1992. It said:

> The gravest threat to the security of India is from the emergence of Pakistan as a nuclear weapon country. Pakistan - aids and abets terrorism in Jammu and Kashmir, Punjab and Assam and promotes infiltration into Gujarat, Kutch and the border districts of Rajasthan and also engages in smuggling and trafficking in drugs. Two years ago, the President of Pakistan referred to Kashmir as the unfinished business of the partition. Early this week, the same President declared that Kashmir belongs to Pakistan and Pakistan will not rest until it takes over Kashmir.
>
> Pakistan will come to terms emotionally with India only when it clearly perceives that continued hostility towards India will bring about its own destruction. Unfortunately, for over four decades India's foreign and defence policies have been lacking in clarity and are devoid of understanding of objective conditions of the world. India did not wake up when China, after humiliating her in 1962, went on to become a nuclear weapon power in 1964. Even now in the light of Pakistan emerging as a nuclear weapon state, while the BJP has demanded that India must exercise its nuclear option so as to meet any threat to its security, there is evidence that the Government of India is under heavy pressure to give up the option. The BJP would like to alert the nation about the perfunctory approach of the Government of India in this matter.

The resolution quoted above went on make the following comments on India's nuclear option:

> The BJP has been known and respected for its no-nonsense approach to the preservation of India's unity and territorial integrity which means *inter alia* security from external threats. The BJP calls upon the Government of India not only not to give up the nuclear option under any circumstances but to exercise the option immediately. Further there must be no delay in the testing and development of the 'Agni' missile.

The party also commented very strongly on the extension and ratification of the Non-Proliferation Treaty. The party refused to accept the theses that while national security of some countries required the continuation of nuclear tests, the others would not be allowed to do so. The party categorically rejected this philosophy of 'Nuclear apartheid'. In his address at the plenary session of the party on November 10, 1995, LK Advani said:

> We regard the NPT and its recent extension and ratification as an iniquitous arrangement. We believe that a Comprehensive Test Ban Treaty can be arrived at but not through the creation of 'nuclear apartheid'. We cannot recognise that thesis which advocates different treatment for the national interests of one, and a totally different yardstick for others.
>
> Whilst the BJP reaffirms its commitment to a global and total eradication of all weapons of mass destruction, till such time as such an arrangement can be convincingly brought about, India must reserve to itself the right to take all such decisions as are in the interest of the nation. We urge upon this government, therefore, to join with us in giving expression to precisely this thought from the sovereign platform of our Parliament.
>
> So far as the BJP is concerned, it would like to reiterate its view that against the background of both China and Pakistan having become nuclear powers,

national security warrants that India, too, must develop a nuclear deterrent of its own.

In view of the continued pressure on the Government of India by the United States and other major powers to give up its nuclear option, the BJP took up this question in December 23, 1995 meeting of the National Executive. The party reiterated its conviction that India's security could not be assured without the possession of nuclear weapons. The party resolution stated:

> The BJP deplores the tendency of the US Administration to pressurise India to give up its sovereign rights and meekly submit to foreign interests. It is India's sovereign right to determine what is necessary to assure its security, unity and territorial integrity.
>
> The BJP demands that Government of India clearly state that it will not accede to a Comprehensive Test Ban Treaty (CTBT) nor agree to a fissile materials cut-off for weapons purposes nor accept the provisions of the discriminatory Missile Technology Control Rêgime (MTCR) until and unless a treaty is established for the total elimination of nuclear weapons universally within a stipulated time-frame. For the Government of India to do otherwise would mean accepting the concept of nuclear apartheid with the BJP vehemently rejects.

Bangladesh Infiltration

The BJP has always viewed the large-scale and continuing infiltration of Bangladeshis into India as a serious threat to peace and harmony in our polity. The party considered it most unfortunate that the Government of India and that of West Bengal had not taken adequate action to put an end to this silent demographic invasion. It noted that their interest lied like in using Bangladeshis to enlarge their vote-bank. The BJP called upon the nation to take serious note of the problem and force the authorities to look at it from the angle of national security rather than political expediency. The BJP repeatedly drew attention of the Government and the People of India to the threat that Bangladeshis infiltration posed to the security of India.

In a resolution adopted at the National Executive meeting on September 8, 1992, the BJP said that the government in West Bengal had admitted large-scale infiltration after pretending for years that there was none. The Government admitted this only when infiltrators in Calcutta turned out in a procession in large numbers demanding citizenship. The party regretted they were not lover arrested. The party resolution went on to make the following significant remarks:

> Communal organisations like Jamat-e-Islami and Islamic Sewa Sangh have very strong clout with these infiltrators. These outfits are constantly injecting the communal virus in the social fabric of North-Eastern India. Virulent propaganda to aid and abet the secessionist forces is continuously carried out by these elements. Literature supporting the formation of an independent 'Greater Bang' including Bangladesh, West Bengal, Assam, North-Eastern states and parts of Bihar and Orissa is being circulated. Bangladeshi leaders are openly advocating the demand of a 'labensraum'. Reports of ULFA making a common cause with the United Minority Front of Assam – a political party founded by the pro-infiltrator lobby under the leadership of Golam Osmani have widely appeared. After Bangladesh proclaimed Islam as the State religion the plight of Hindus, Sikhs, Buddhists and Christians became miserable. They were denied all civic and cultural rights and were forced to leave their homes in order to save their lives and honour. Under the United Nations Commission on refugees, these persons taking refuge in India are to be treated as refugees. While infiltrators have been given all facilities, these refugees are denied even ration cards. The Government of India

has miserably failed in seeking protection for them in Bangladesh and has never raised this question of violation of human rights either in the international forums or even with Begum Khalida Zia when she visited India. The government has bungled on this issue of continued influx of infiltrators by not raising this subject during the discussions with the Bangladeshi Prime Minister. Such is the perfunctory attitude of the Central Government on this question affecting our security.

The BJP expresses its grave concern at the total indifference of the Government of India as well as the State Governments of West Bengal, Assam, Tripura, Manipur and Bihar towards this problem, which could be ignored and evaded only at national peril.

United States and Pakistan

The BJP expressed its shock and resentment that despite the end of the Cold War there continues to be a pro-Pakistan tilt in the American policy towards the Indian subcontinent. At one time, there were some indications that the United States was getting ready to put Pakistan on its watch list of promoters of terrorism. But this did not come about and the United States supported Pakistan's designs on Kashmir by declaring that the whole State was disputed territory. In a resolution adopted at the National Executive meeting on June 9, 1994, the BJP charged that the United States adopted pro-Pakistan and anti-Indian postures. It said:

> The US is preparing to reward Pakistan for its development of nuclear weapons of which the US intelligence agencies were fully aware, by supplying dozens of F-16 aircraft which, with some modification, can bombard large parts of India with nuclear weapons. At the same time, it threatens India with dire consequences if it continued to retain its nuclear option and proceeds with the development of the 'Agni' missile and deployment of 'Prithvi' missiles.

No wonder Pakistan feels it can come to no harm by continuing to aid and abet the terrorists in Jammu and Kashmir. At the same time, despite its dismal performance in Geneva at the annual session of the UN Human Rights Commission held earlier this year, Pakistan has not abandoned its efforts to internationalise the Kashmir question in the guise of protection of the human rights of the people of Kashmir. There are credible reports to suggest that Pakistan will once again attempt in the UN General Assembly to pass an anti-Indian resolution. The reports also suggest that Pakistan will attempt to debate the question in the UN Security Council before the end of the year. Thus, the instigator of terrorism, Pakistan, will attempt to put the victim, India, in the dock in various international fora.

Israel

The BJP welcomed the establishment of diplomatic relations with Israel in 1992. The party had maintained for a long-time that India must establish ties with Israel, as that would be beneficial to India for several reasons. The party had repressed in main that it did not serve India's diplomatic interests to shun Israel while extending full support to the Palestine cause. There was room for India to build the country that they can have both sides to resolve their differences. The party believed that maintaining and good relations with Israel will help India in developing both relations with the United States.

MANIFESTOES OF 1996 AND 1998

BJP's Foreign Policy Goals

After 15 years of its existence, the BJP had a clear vision of its objectives in the sphere of foreign policy. In the manifestoes of 1996 and 1998, the party clearly reflected the targets it wished to achieve. These two documents became the basis of the policies subsequently pursued by the party when it came to power in April 1998. The earlier period of two weeks, in 1996, when Atal Bihari Vajpayee became Prime Minister for a fortnight was too short for any significant policy moves.

The party noted that in a post-Cold War world, India would be confronted by many new challenges and opportunities. It expressed its readiness to meet those challenges and in doing so, it was determined to abide by the human values of peace, equality and cooperation.

The BJP felt rather strongly that in the preceding years, India had not been able to assert its position in the comity of nations. It said in its 1996 manifesto -

> The BJP holds that as a departure from the recent past, Indian diplomacy should be conducted in tune with India's position as a strong power and a major player in the world arena. A billion people, who do not depend upon anyone for feeding or clothing themselves are a power, which cannot be ignored. Our nation needs to regain its lost pride and the BJP alone can undertake this task. While we believe in partnership with everyone, we reject the very thought of patronage by anybody.

Likewise, the 1995 manifesto included the following statement:

> In the recent past, we have seen a tendency to bend under pressure. This arises as much out of ignorance of our rightful place and role in world affairs as also from a loss of national self-confidence and resolve. A nation as large and capable as ourselves must make its impact felt on the world arena. BJP government will demand a premier position for the country in all global fora.

The BJP expressed regret and dismay on the unfortunate neglect of matters relating to national security. It clearly stated its intention to establish a National Security Council to constantly analyse security, political and economic threats and render continuous advice to the government. This

Council will undertake India's first-ever Strategic Defence Review to study and analyse the security environment and make appropriate recommendations to cover all aspects of defence requirements and organisations.

The BJP had maintained for a long time that production of nuclear weapons by India was absolutely essential unless the nuclear weapon powers agreed to an international treaty to reduce and eventually abolish all nuclear weapons. Since there were no moves in this direction, the party was considered opinion that India should have its own nuclear deterrent. The party manifesto of 1998, therefore, very clearly stated that the party would re-evaluate the country's nuclear policy and exercise the option to induct nuclear weapons. At the same time, the party also pledged to expedite the development of the 'Agni' series ballistic missiles.

The BJP categorically rejected the motion of nuclear apartheid and stated that it will actively oppose attempts to impose hegemonic nuclear regime by means of CTBT, FMCF and MTCR. It asserted that it would not be dictated to by anybody in matters of security requirements and in the exercise of nuclear option.

Among other things, the BJP foreign policy agenda included the following prominent objections:

1. To give India a role and position in world affairs commensurate with its size and capability.
2. To promote sovereign equality among nations, the BJP rejects all forms of political and economic hegemonism and is committed to actively resisting such efforts.
3. To vigorously pursue endeavours for India to become a permanent member of the United Nations Security Council. We believe that the existing arrangements in the UN are tilted in the favour of certain countries to serve their narrow interest.
4. To re-orient Indian diplomacy to our economic and commercial goals and to ensure that our missions

abroad play a more active and supportive role in meting these.

5. To promote greater regional and civilisational relationship and strive for Asian solidarity in general and the development of the South Asian Association for Regional Cooperation in particular.
6. To place relations with the USA on a more even platform based on mutual respect, shared values and congruence of interests. We expect the United States to be more sensitive to India's security and economic interests.
7. To take active steps to persuade Pakistan to abandon its present policy of hostile interference in our internal affairs by supporting insurgent and terrorist groups. The BJP affirms unequivocally India's sovereignty over the whole of Jammu and Kashmir, including the areas under foreign occupations.
8. To improve relations with China by seeking speedy resolution of the outstanding border problem. Even while doing so we will seek greater cross-border trade and cooperation in other areas. We are also concerned about China continuing transfer of advanced weapons and technologies to Pakistan as this has a vital bearing on our ties with China.
9. To maintain the unique, warm and friendly relations with Nepal with which India has the closest cultural, religious and historical ties.

NDA REGIME

The exemplary conduct of foreign affairs was a major success story of the BJP-led National Democratic Alliance government during the period 1998-2004. Under the dynamic leadership of Atal Bihari Vajpayee, the fossilised foreign policy of the preceding Governments was transformed into a vibrant instrument for the promotion of India's vital interests in the international arena. Because of the foreign policy achievements of that period, India today enjoys a much higher status in the world community than it ever did since Independence.

India's international standing had fallen abysmally low during the 1990s. A few instances would suffice to recall the pitiable state of India's international status at that point of time. India failed to win an election to one of the non-permanent seats in the Security Council and could muster only 42 votes despite the massive campaign launched to win the election. The organisers of the Europe-Asia summit did not consider it necessary to invite India to this international gathering. Even our neighbouring countries cared very little for India's interests and some were actually quite hostile. This was happening despite the so-called Gujral doctrine, essentially a very noble idea of making concessions to smaller neighbours in the hope of improving relations but in fact it led to quite the opposite. Smaller neighbours began to interpret this as India's weakness and tried to take undue advantage.

India's defence forces at that time were suffering from lack of proper equipment and resources. Nuclear policy was in shambles. Some attempts to develop nuclear weapons were thwarted by the nuclear powers using various means. The unstable Governments of the '90s had buckled under pressure and threats of economic and other sanctions.

One of the first major actions of the Vajpayee government to strengthen India's national security was to exercise the nuclear option. India had this option for many years but no government could muster enough courage to turn this option into reality. The BJP had maintained that in the given international situation, development and induction of nuclear weapons into our security system was absolutely essential.

The nuclear tests were conducted on May 11 and May 13, 1998. The National Executive of the BJP hailed the successful nuclear tests conducted by the BJP-led government as a bold and decisive step in the right direction. Pokhran-II had not only demonstrated that India's indigenous talent is second to none but also provided the nation with a nuclear deterrent.

The BJP's views on nuclear policy were expressed in the resolution adopted at the National Executive of the party on August 21. It said:

> The BJP subscribes to the view that lasting global peace can be achieved and the threat of nuclear war eliminated only when nuclear weapon states adopt and implement a time-bound programme to dismantle their weapons of mass destruction. But so long as these states continue to stockpile weapons, it serves so long as these states continue to stockpile weapons, it serves little purpose and works against India's security interests to renounce nuclear deterrence capability.
>
> As expected, economic measures have been taken against India for daring to challenge discriminatory arrangements. But India's spirit cannot be broken by sanctions or by initiating punitive steps like the expulsion of Indian scientists working in research establishments. India has the strength and the capacity to withstand and survive economic sanctions.
>
> The National Executive welcomes the unilateral moratorium on further tests but urges the Government to review this decision if future developments jeopardize national strategic and security interests. We urge the government to bear in mind that India stayed out of the CTBT in 1996 because of national security concerns and the discriminatory character of the Treaty. The same principle should guide any dialogue on India becoming a signatory to any multilateral control regime.
>
> We also welcome the Government's post-Pokharan diplomatic initiative that has enabled many foreign Governments to realise that India has genuine security concerns and that these concerns need to be addressed. India, contrary to what the BJP-led Government's critics claim, is neither isolated nor cornered following the tests; India has emerged as a confident sovereign state, sure of its place in the comity of nations.

As mentioned earlier, national security, national integrity and national interest are the three main planks that continue to shape the BJP's foreign policy. Considerations of national security necessitated the development of a nuclear deterrent. The initial adverse international reaction was handled with great aplomb. A sustained dialogue with the major players convinced the international community that Indian security concerns required the acquisition of a viable minimum deterrent. Within a short span, we were able to transform the strained relationship with major powers into friendly, cooperative and meaningful relationship.

The NDA government evolved a nuclear doctrine, which clearly lays down that India's nuclear weapons are only for defensive purposes and that India will adhere steadfastly to the concept of no first use of nuclear weapons. Similarly, India will continue to abide by accepted international norms on non-proliferation of nuclear technology. India has clearly emerged as a responsible nuclear power.

Neighbouring Countries

The second most important foreign policy issue before the government was relations with the neighbouring countries. The well-meaning Gujral doctrine has proved to be quite inadequate to convert hostility into friendship. It was felt that bilateral relations with the neighbours must be based on some kind of mutuality of interests and must have an element of reciprocity.

The NDA government was able to normalise and improve relations substantially with all the neighbouring countries except Pakistan and to some extent with Bangladesh. The large-scale influx of Bangladeshis into India became a major irritant in Indo-Bangladesh relations. But the more serious concern was the increasing evidence of Islamic Jehadis crossing border from Bangladesh into Indian territory for engaging in terrorists activities.

Pakistan

A major initiative was taken to improve relations with Pakistan when Prime Minister Vajpayee travelled to Lahore in a bus to have a dialogue with Pakistan Prime Minister Nawaz Sharif. This peaceful gesture, however, failed to convince the Pakistani rulers of the need for normalisation of relations between India and Pakistan. They responded, instead, by launching an aggression in the Kargil region in Jammu and Kashmir in May-June 1999.

Two years after, the Kargil conflict, Prime Minister Vajpayee, invited Gen Pervez Musharraf for the Agra Summit. This was an act of statesmanship, reflecting of India's policy of establishing peaceful and normal relations with Pakistan. The Bharatiya Janata Party has always believed that India and Pakistan cannot live in perpetual hostility. The BJP's views on relationship with Pakistan at that point of time were clearly reflected in the following extract form the resolution adopted by the National Executive on July 29, 2001:

> The BJP believes that efforts to improve relations with Pakistan should continue. However, it must be clearly understood that no meaningful dialogue with Pakistan can be conducted as long as the 'jehadi' mentality dominates the Pakistani establishment. There are elements in Pakistan, who interpret India's friendly gestures as a sign of weakness and a proof of the success of the Pakistani-sponsored cross-border terrorism. The BJP would like to such people to know that India's friendly overtures are indicative of our overwhelming and oft-demonstrated strength and also of our innate desire for peace and friendship with all our neighbours. If Pakistan continues to adopt a negative posture, the Government of India should draw appropriate conclusions and plan for the future accordingly.

Several attempts were made, thereafter, to continue to engage in a dialogue with Pakistan. The Pakistani insistence on raising the Kashmir question as the core issue at every opportunity was not helpful at all. Attempts were made to convince the Pakistanis that India will not agree to any further map-making in the subcontinent. Even Pakistani commentators began to point out to President Musharraf that Pakistan who failed to wrest Kashmir from India despite several wars. The UN Resolutions also had not been of any help to Pakistan. Pakistan's attempts to involve third parties into the conflict as an arbitrator had failed and that cross-border terrorism in which Pakistan had engaged for bleeding India had not affected India's progress. But, it had, in fact, ruined Pakistan's economy and brought down her international standing. The Indian side had repeatedly suggested that the two countries should engage in interaction in various fields of activity and put aside the Kashmir question for resolution at a later date. Attempts were made to impress upon the Pakistani interlocutors that once Indo-Pak relation develop in a variety of spheres, a conducive atmosphere will be created for resolving the Kashmir problem. The example of the European Union shows that when countries involve themselves in diverse interactions, the borders began to lose much of their significance. The example of Indo-China relationship was also given. Both countries continue to discuss the border issue, but do not allow it to come in the way of a wide-ranging relationship in all spheres.

As a result of repeated attempts, interaction began to take place between India and Pakistan, in a number of fields and the atmosphere had become much more relaxed. The major gain for India was the signing of a joint statement during Prime Minister Vajpayee's visit to Islamabad in January 2004 under which Pakistan agreed to ensure that Pakistani territory was not used by terrorists for engaging in cross-border terrorism.

International Issues

Soon after the nuclear tests, the NDA government faced prospects of a very hostile reaction from various quarters. Besides the United States, which was most vociferous, the European Union, Japan, China, Australia and many other countries expressed views highly critical of India's action. Several countries individually issued sanctions against India and some of them called upon the international agencies to impose strict sanctions. This was a difficult period, but the government handled the situation admirably. Special envoys were sent to many countries and all Indian diplomatic missions were galvanised to project the Government of India's main point. Within a year, things began to change and most countries accepted that India had genuine security concerns. The International Community began to recognise India's importance as a political and economic power and did not wish to jeopardize their own interests by lowering the level of interaction with India. The era of sanctions, therefore, there was of a very short duration. India's international diplomacy had been a great success.

Terrorism

India had faced terrorist activity for several years before the September 2001 terrorist attacks on New York and Washington. The 9/11 attacks led to universal awareness of the danger from 'jehadi' terrorism. India and United States pledged to fight the scourge of terrorism together. The UN Resolution on the means to fight terrorism was welcomed by the Government of India. India, accordingly strengthen its laws to fight terrorist activities. India also offered its help to the United States to deal with the jehadi forces of al-Qaeda. India supported the US action in Afghanistan against al-Qaeda and Taliban. The Vajpayee Government, however, had some strong reservations about US attack on Iraq. The government felt that unilateral action of the United States was deplorable and that this should have been done with UN approval.

The successful foreign policy of the Vajpayee government was noted by the Bharatiya Janata Party in its National Executive Resolution of November 26, 2004 in the following words:

> Among the many sterling achievements of the Vajpayee Government, the successful conduct of foreign policy was the most outstanding. The Vajpayee government, guided only by supreme national interest, conducted nuclear tests soon after coming to power in 1998. Therefore, it successfully overcame the opposition of leading global powers to this move. It also resolutely and successfully met the challenge of economic sanctions imposed by these countries. Its diplomacy was so consummate that the end of its tenure in 2004. India was on the high table of all international gatherings was widely respected and several important and new initiatives were taken on all fronts. The most notable, of course, were the initiatives to resolve the outstanding issues with China and Pakistan, the establishment of a healthy and fruitful relationship with the USA, the EU, Russia, Japan, ASEAN and other countries. It initiated determined steps to improve and intensify its relationship with its neighbours. The peace initiative with Pakistan, was a particular, of historic significance as was the Joint Press Statement issued after Prime Minister Vajpayee's meeting, with President Musharraf, in Islamabad, on 6th January, 2004.

The Vajpayee era of 1998 to 2004 witnessed a very substantial transformation of Indian foreign policy. The old era of the pursuit of outdated ideologies had given way to the pursuit of national interest. Pragmatism, practicality and reason played the dominant part in determining Indian relations with other countries. As the National Security advisor stated at an international conference:

> India takes decisions on the basis of national interest and no longer accepts unquestioningly the doctrines of non-violence and non-alignment.

Those policies were grounded in strict rationality and real politic. They were not relevant any more. India had moved on from idealism to pragmatism. This transformation necessitated a change in India's relations with the outside world. Rapid economic development was essential to make India a strong and prosperous nation. This necessitated a new stress on economics in the making of foreign policy. The socialist era had come to an end and a sustained engagement with the capitalist world was called for. A good example was the India-US dialogue, which helped change bilateral relations steadily and quite deeply. Similar dialogues were mediated with a number of major players.

The BJP government gave a new and healthy direction to Indian foreign policy.

Looking at the Future

The 21st century, they say, is going to be Asia's century just as the 19th century was a European century and the 20th century was an American century. Japan has already moved into the big league and both China and India are not far behind. With the Asian countries taking a leap forward, Asian resurgence is very much on the horizon. However, for the near future, the United States and Europe are expected to dominate the international scene. Despite its present, dominating military and economic prowess, the US is unlikely to wish away a multilateral world. The BJP expects a multipolar world to emerge in the near future with India as one of its important poles. The International Community cannot do away with a United Nations structure but the institution needs a restructuring in which India must play an important part. The world is rapidly becoming a global village and many issues which were hither to considered a national concern are now acquiring an international character. We must create an awareness among our people about the need for a broad-minded approach to a variety of issues and to take greater interest in international affairs.

Terrorism has emerged as a major threat to the civilised world. The BJP would like India to collaborate with all nations to root out this evil from the international scene. Islamic nations must be persuaded to find ways and means of controlling elements which engage in terrorism in the name of Islam.

With the world recognising India as an emerging power, our foreign policy has to become far more active, creative and sure-footed. The NDA government had launched a number of bold initiatives during its regime and there is an urgent need to build upon those policy innovations. Unfortunately, the UPA government has reversed some of those steps and we hope that correction will be applied soon.

BJP's foreign policy vision of the coming years includes the following:

1. Strengthening the forces of multilateralism. The United Nations Organisation needs to be strengthened and restructured. The realities of the present day international situation must be taken into account while giving shape to this august body. India must play an important role in the UN and other multilateral institutions, both international and regional.
2. Carrying forward vigorously the Look East Policy pursued by the NDA government. Previous Governments have tended to neglect this region, which should in fact, be part of our extended neighbourhood. More vigorous interaction with the Asian countries, China and Japan will enable us to strengthen Asian solidarity.
3. Raising the level of interaction with the European Union. The EU has emerged as an economically strong and powerful entity. There is a continuing and regular interaction between India and some countries of the EU as also an annual Indo-EU

Summit. This has proved to be very beneficial for India's economic development and our politico-strategic interests. The BJP would like to see the development of stronger bonds with the EU as a whole as also with individual members of the European Union.

4. Forging closer relations with the United States in all spheres. In recent years, India and the US have moved away from the past estrangement to a very positive engagement. The BJP believes that India and the US are natural allies and that cooperation and understanding between these two largest democracies in the world would not only promote their mutual benefit but will also contribute towards peace and prosperity in the world.
5. Developing extensive contacts with countries of Africa and South America. The BJP recognises that there are various kinds of impediments in establishing a meaningful relationship with these countries, but strongly believes that the difficulties can be overcome to create new linkages. The developing countries have had a raw deal in the past and must look for new arrangements and new organisations for protection of their economic and political interests.
6. Re-fashioning the traditional relations with Russia and the Central Asian countries. During the Soviet era, our relationship with these countries was quite extensive and we have developed links which can be used for mutual benefit in the coming years, especially in the economic sphere.
7. Carrying forward the dialogue with Pakistan to normalise relations between the two countries. We believe that India and Pakistan must work together to build a bright future for the South Asia region. A continuous dialogue and a step-by-step approach

will help in resolving all outstanding issues between India and Pakistan. Improved relations between the two countries will help in rejuvenating the SAARC. If Pakistan continues to adopt a negative approach, India should go ahead with sub-regional and bilateral economic cooperation with the other members of SAARC.

8. Paying special attention to the promising economic relationship with West Asian countries. We have historical links with this region. It is also an energy rich area and should be an integral part of our long-term plans for India' energy security.
9. Strengthening further the existing close-relationship with Nepal and Bhutan, our most intimate neighbours, for mutual benefit. They have helped India in combating terrorist activities. We have assisted them in their economic development and will continue to do in future.
10. Watching carefully the developments in Afghanistan and Iraq. We have had an extensive relationship with both these countries in the past. The BJP is happy that India has been associated with the task of reconstruction of Afghanistan. We would be willing to render all possible assistance to Iraq. We would like to see Iraq emerge as a democratic and pluralist society.
11. Maintaining close contacts with people of Indian origin settled abroad. The NDA government has already taken several steps to promote regular interaction with the Non-Resident Indians. January is being celebrated every year as 'Pravasi Divas'. Awards have been instituted for the people of Indian origin abroad. The demand of the PIOs for dual nationality has been agreed to. We will continue to take further measures to ensure that the PIOs get every opportunity to participate in India's march towards prosperity and strength.

INDIA-US RELATIONS

In the post-Cold War world, Vajpayee boosted trade and bilateral relations with the US leading to the historic visit in 2000 by Bill Clinton, who became the first American President to visit India since Jimmy Carter in 1978. Besides promoting economic ties between India and China, his government also initiated a structured mechanism for high-level dialogue to resolve the border dispute between the two countries. Vajpayee's 'Look East' policy helped in improving India's ties with countries in South-East Asia and East Asia.

Many were caught by surprise when Vajpayee first declared that India and the US, the world's largest and oldest democracies, were natural allies. Foreign affairs expert Stephen P Cohen wrote:

> The Vajpayee government invented the term 'natural alliance' which has been adopted by Prime Minister (Manmohan) Singh's government, and American officials."

In his 2000 address to the US Congress, Vajpayee said India and the US had taken a decisive step away from the past. He said:

> The dawn of the new century has marked a new beginning in our relations.

Clinton signalled Washington's shift from its close ties with Islamabad, while Vajpayee showed India's willingness to no longer be as reliant as before on Russia. It was that landmark document that laid the platform for his successors Manmohan Singh and Modi to build on and turn the bilaterals into one of the most robust ones in India's foreign policy network. Vajpayee can be credited with putting the India-US relations on course for the strategic partnership that exists today.

INDIA-CHINA RELATIONS

In 2003 Prime Minister Vajpayee was invited by then Premier of China Wen Jiabao for a milestone State visit and it culminated in the signing of a Declaration on Principles for Relations and Comprehensive Cooperation. Within this text, were the lines:

> The common interests of the two sides outweigh their differences. The two countries are not a threat to each other. Neither side shall use or threaten to use force against the other.... Both sides agree to qualitatively enhancing the bilateral relationship at all levels and in all areas while addressing differences through peaceful means in a fair, reasonable and mutually acceptable manner. The differences should not be allowed to affect the overall development of bilateral relations.

And since then, all sorts of ministerial and special representatives' consultations have been put in place between the two countries, not to mention the array of multilateral institutions that number both countries as members.

INDIA-PAKISTAN RELATIONS

Dealing with Pakistan was more challenging although Vajpayee consistently maintained that stopping cross-border infiltration and destruction of terrorist infrastructure by Pakistan could open the doors for talks. "Talks can take place on all issues, including that of Jammu and Kashmir," he said.

When he took over as PM, cross-border terrorism was rampant, but much to India's discomfiture, world powers then were not ready to support New Delhi's contention that Pakistan was sponsoring terror outfits to carry out attacks on India. Against heavy odds, he sought normalisation of ties with Pakistan, reasoning that one can change friends, but had to live with one's neighbours.

In 1999, Vajpayee made his historic bus journey to Lahore in quest of peace. "The partition of our country had caused a wound in our heart, that wound had healed and the mark left by it reminds us that we have to live in harmony with one another," Vajpayee said at a civic reception in Lahore in February 1999.

Foreign policy under Vajpayee saw many innovations, particularly his attempts to reset India-Pakistan ties. An agreement to launch an India-Pakistan bus link connecting New Delhi to Lahore was signed in 1999. Vajpayee himself travelled to Pakistan on the inaugural service and the two sides signed a pact agreeing to inform each other ahead of missile tests as a major confidence building measure.

Having made good on the promise to move India away from nuclear ambiguity since the Pokhran test of 1974, Vajpayee unilaterally committed to two important stabilizing measures: an informal moratorium on further nuclear tests and a commitment to 'No First Use' of nuclear weapons. India has not resumed nuclear testing despite not being a party to the Comprehensive Nuclear Test Ban Treaty. And by committing to 'No First Use' posture, India has simultaneously introduced a measure of crisis stability in the South Asian subcontinent as well as prevented an all-out arms race in the region. Both pillars have also been paramount in securing India's entry into the global nuclear and non-proliferation order despite not being an NPT (Non-Proliferation Treaty) signatory.

India's conduct during the Kargil War of 1999 is also a testament to strategic restraint – and the rich dividends that it sometimes pays. In May 1999, the Pakistani military decided to avenge India's 1984 occupation of the Siachen glacier through a *fait accompli* in the Kargil-Dras sector of Jammu and Kashmir. It is almost certain that the presence of nuclear weapons on both sides emboldened the Pakistani military to upset the *status quo* without fears of an Indian reprisal. What ensued – one of only two limited wars between nuclear powers – was a demonstration of Indian resolve as well as restraint. Vajpayee made it clear, early on in the conflict, that India will not cede any territory or accept a ceasefire unless Pakistan's forces had vacated the peaks of Kargil. At the same time, he issued firm instructions to the Indian Armed Forces, notably to the Indian Air Force, not to breach the LoC. Tactically, this would translate to extremely careful manoeuvring by the IAF. However, had India breached the LoC, it would have been held responsible for expanding the conflict. In that case, India would not have been able to generate a favourable international intercession, which ultimately became the case.

Vajpayee's approach to China also illustrated his keen ability to balance contending impulses in international politics. Despite the Jana Sangh's suspicion of China, as Moraji Desai's Foreign Minister, Vajpayee became the first Indian cabinet minister to visit China in two decades. What transpired in his meetings with his then counterpart Huang Hua is in itself interesting. February 1979 Press Trust of India interview with Huang has the minister describing the meeting: "Mr Vajpayee stated that the boundary issue should not constitute a hindrance to the improvement of our bilateral relations." This approach of India continues to serve as a template despite the Doklam standoff last year. This, however, did not make Vajpayee any less aware of the challenges of Chinese power.

Having established notional nuclear parity with China in 1998, Vajpayee began a high-profile outreach, which included a visit to Beijing in 2003. India's official recognition of the Tibetan Autonomous Region as part of mainland China, Vajpayee also instituted Special Representatives mechanism for resolving the border dispute between the two countries. By appointing his Principal Secretary and National Security Adviser Brajesh Mishra as the first Special Representatives, Vajpayee instituted the first high-level mechanism in decades to address the long-standing problem.

Ultimately, a lot of the fruit of Vajpayee's labour in the realm of foreign policy is being borne today/will be borne in the years to come. His disruption of the Cold War order and broadening of India's international relations horizons were responsible for sowing foreign policy seeds that remain the former Prime Minister's biggest contribution to India's foreign policy.

3

Golden Quadrilateral

The Golden Quadrilateral or "GQ" was former Prime Minister Atal Bihari Vajpayee's first dream project and is enshrined as the biggest infrastructure intervention in the roadways sector in post-Independent India, making 5,846 kms of highways.

"Atalji used to say 'humaare desh mein sadkon mein gaddhe hain ya gaddhon mein sadke hain?' (Does our country have potholes on roads or roads in potholes?)," recalled LK Joshi, who was Member, NHAI, during this time and later became Secretary, Ministry of Road Transport and Highways. "So the first chance he got, he sanctioned "GQ", his greatest contribution to infrastructure in India.

Within months of assuming charge as Prime Minister in 1999, Vajpayee called a meeting in the PMO to direct the Road Transport Ministry to map out "20 most congested areas of India" and make a plan to create four-lane highways to ease congestion, officials recalled. What emerged was the grand design to connect Delhi, Mumbai, Kolkata and Chennai for seamless movement of freight. The work started in less than a year. Prime Minister Atal Bihari Vajpayee laid the foundation stone for the project on 6 January 1999. To fund the grand project, Vajpayee recast the Central Road Fund, a fund traditionally made out of cess on the sale of petrol and diesel. Eventually, the complete GQ with not just north-south and east-west corridors but the diagonal arms through the first two phases of NHDP cost ₹ 64,639 crore. The original plan of the GQ stood completed by 2012. "The pace of work was such that 90% of the original GQ plan was implemented within four years," said a senior ministry official.

The GQ brought in many firsts for India's highways sector. It laid roads with Hot Mix Plants for bitumen for the first time; medians were introduced as a matter of design, safety features like guardrails were incorporated; and the process included bringing consultants from outside for engineering solutions. An equally significant contribution of his in bolstering the country's infrastructure is the Pradhan Mantri Gram Sadak Yojana (PMGSY) (Chapter 4), a project to construct all-weather rural road connectivity, launched in 2000. On date it has been able to cover more than 80% of its original target.

In January 2012, India announced the four-lane GQ highway network as complete.

India's government had initially estimated that the Golden Quadrilateral project would cost ₹ 600 billion (US $ 8.7 billion) at 1999 prices. However, the highway has been built under-budget. As of August 2011, cost incurred by Indian government was about half of initial estimate, at ₹ 308.58 billion (US $ 4.5 billion). The eight contracts in progress, as on August 2011, were worth ₹ 16.34 billion (US $ 240 million).

In September 2009, it was announced that the existing four-laned highways would be converted into six-lane highways. The expansion project was reported at various stages to be behind schedule, mainly due to land acquisition constraints and disputes with contractors which had to be re-negotiated.

Sections of NH 2, NH 5 and NH 8 have now been prioritized for further widening to six lanes under DBFO (Design, Build, Finance, Operate) pattern and more sections would be six-laned in the near future. On NH 8 six-lane work is completed from Vadodara to Surat.

The Hosur-Krishnagiri stretch of the Bengaluru-Chennai stretch is being expanded from four lanes to six lanes by Reliance Infrastructure.

The Golden Quadrilateral is a highway network connecting many of the major industrial, agricultural and cultural centres of India. It forms a quadrilateral connecting Chennai, Kolkata, Delhi and Mumbai. Other cities connected by this network are Ahmedabad, Bengaluru, Bhubaneswar, Cuttack, Jaipur, Kanpur, Pune, Surat, Vijayawada, Ajmer, and Vizag, Bodhgaya, Varanasi, Agra, Pune, Dhanbad, Gandhinagar, Kanpur, Udaipur, Pune

It is the largest highway project in India and the fifth longest in the world, at 5,846 km. Started by the NDA government led by Prime Minister Atal Bihari Vajpayee it is the first phase of the National Highways Development Project (NHDP), and consists of 5,846 kms four/six lane express highways, built at a cost of ₹600 billion (US $8.7 billion). The project was launched in 2001 by Atal Bihari Vajpayee, and was completed in 2012. The vast majority of system is not access controlled, although safety features such as guardrails, shoulders, and high-visibility signs are in use.

The Golden Quadrilateral project is managed by the National Highways Authority of India (NHAI) under the Ministry of Road, Transport and Highways. The Mumbai-Pune Expressway, the first controlled-access toll road to be built in India, is a part of the GQ Project but not funded by NHAI, and separate from the main highway. Infrastructure Leasing & Financial Services (IL&FS) has been one of the major contributors to the infrastructural development activity in the GQ project. This project was conceptualised in 1999 and started in 2001. It was projected to connect four metropolitan cities of India: Delhi, Mumbai, Chennai and Kolkata. The project consisted of constructing four- and six-lane express highways. Although the project was planned to be completed by 2006, due to delays like land acquisition, awarding contracts, zoning challenges, and funding problems, it was finally completed in 2012. It is a network of highways that connect the four major metropolitan cities of the country in four directions - Delhi (North), Chennai (South), Kolkata (East) and Mumbai (West) - thereby forming a quadrilateral, and hence the name Golden Quadrilateral.

The planning for the project was completed in 1999 but the construction work officially started in 2001. Though it was estimated to be completed by 2006, it actually became operational in January 2012. The Golden Quadrilateral project included construction of new express highways, including renovation and extension of the existing highways to four or six lanes.

The four sections of the Golden Quadrilateral:

Section I

This section covers a distance of 1,454 kms on national highway 2 (NH2) from Delhi to Kolkata and passes through Delhi, Haryana, Uttar Pradesh, Bihar, Jharkhand and West Bengal, with its major cities being Delhi, Mathura, Faridabad, Agra, Allahabad, Firozabad, Kanpur and Varanasi.

Section II

Stretching about 1,684 kms, this section covers NH6 (Kolkata to Chennai), NH60 (Kharagpur to Balasore) and NH5 (Balasore to Chennai) and passes through West Bengal, Orissa, Telangana, Andhra Pradesh, and Tamil Nadu, and even in parts of Kerala.

Section III

Total stretch of 1,290 kms covering parts of NH4 (Mumbai to Bangalore), NH7 (Bangalore to Krishnagiri, Tamil Nadu) and NH46 (Krishnagiri to near Chennai). It passes through Maharashtra, Karnataka, Andhra Pradesh and Tamil Nadu.

Section IV

Covering parts of NH8 (Delhi to Kishangarh), NH79A (Ajmer bypass), NH79 (Nasirabad to Chittaurgarh) and NH76 (Chittaurgarh to Udaipur), the total length of section IV is 1,419 kms. It passes through the states of Maharashtra, Gujarat, Rajasthan, Haryana and New Delhi, connecting Delhi, Ajmer, Udaipur, Gurgaon, Jaipur, Gandhinagar, Ahmedabad, Vadodara, Surat and Mumbai.

Overall, the Golden Quadrilateral passes through 13 states of India. The Golden Quadrilateral constitutes only the national highways of the country and not state highways and rural-urban roadways.

Economic Benefits

The projected economic benefits of the Golden Quadrilateral project are –

1. Establishing faster transport networks between major cities and ports.
2. Providing an impetus to smoother movement of products and people within India.
3. Enabling industrial and job development in smaller towns through access to markets.
4. Providing opportunities for farmers, through better transportation of produce from the agricultural hinterland to major cities and ports for export, through lesser wastage and spoils.
5. Driving economic growth directly through construction as well as through indirect demand for cement, steel and other construction materials.
6. Giving an impetus to truck transport throughout India.

Route

Only National Highways are used in the Golden Quadrilateral. The four legs use the following National Highways (New Numbering System):

- Delhi - Kolkata: NH 19
- Delhi - Chennai: NH 48
- Kolkata - Chennai: NH 16

Important Cities Connected by Golden Quadrilateral Highway

Delhi – Kolkata

(1) Delhi, (2) Faridabad, (3) Mathura, (4) Agra, (5) Firozabad, (6) Etawah, (7) Kanpur, (8) Fatehpur district, (9) Allahabad, (10) Varanasi, (11) Chandauli, (12) Mohania, (13) Kudra, (14) Sasaram, (15) Dehri, (16) Aurangabad, (17) Sherghati, (18) Dobhi, (19) Chouparan, (20) Barhi, (21) Ishri, (22) Bagodar, (23) Dhanbad, (24) Asansol, (25) Durgapur, (26) Bardhaman, (27) Kolkata

Kolkata – Chennai

(1) Kolkata, (2) Kharagpur, (3) Balasore, (4) Cuttack, (5) Bhubaneswar, (6) Visakhapatnam, (7) Rajahmundry, (8) Eluru, (9) Vijayawada, (10) Guntur, (11) Nellore, (12) Chennai

Chennai – Mumbai

(1) Chennai, (2) Sriperumbudur, (3) Kanchipuram, (4) Walajapet, (5) Ranipet, (6) Vellore, (7) Pallikonda, (8) Ambur, (9) Vaniyambadi, (10) Krishnagiri, (11) Hosur, (12) Bengaluru, (13) Tumakuru, (14) Sira, (15) Chitradurga, (16) Davangere, (17) Ranebennur, (18) Hubballi-Dharwad, (19) Belagavi, (20) Kolhapur, (21) Sangli-Miraj, (22) Karad, (23) Satara, (24) Pune, (25) Panvel, (26) Mumbai

Mumbai – Delhi

(1) Mumbai, (2) Silvassa, (3) Vapi, (4) Valsad, (5) Navsari, (6) Surat, (7) Bharuch, (8) Ankleshwar, (9) Vadodara,

(10) Anand, (11) Nadiad, (12) Ahmedabad, (13) Gandhinagar, (14) Udaipur, (15) Chittaurgarh, (16) Ajmer, (17) Jaipur, (18) Gurgaon, (19) Delhi

Length in Each State

The completed Golden Quadrilateral passes through 13 states:

- Andhra Pradesh - 1,014 kms
- Uttar Pradesh - 756 kms
- Rajasthan - 725 kms
- Karnataka - 623 kms
- Maharashtra - 487 kms
- Gujarat - 485 kms
- Odisha - 440 kms
- West Bengal - 406 kms
- Tamil Nadu - 342 kms
- Bihar - 204 kms
- Jharkhand - 192 kms
- Haryana - 152 kms
- Delhi - 25 kms
- Total - 5,846 kms

NDA's plan was to showcase GQ as an example of Indian highways attaining global standards while boosting local economies around it. Though it was estimated to be completed by 2006, it actually became operational in January 2012. Projects have been delayed mainly due to problems associated with land acquisition, shifting of utilities, obtaining environment and forest clearance, approval for road over bridges, poor performance of some contractors due to cash flow constraints and law and order problems in some states. The project has been executed through a Public-Private Partnership (PPP) between the NHAI and the corresponding contractors. The contractors will collect the toll taxes for a specified concession period.

4

Pradhan Mantri Gram Sadak Yojana

Introduction

Rural Road Connectivity is not only a key component of Rural Development by promoting access to economic and social services and thereby generating increased agricultural incomes and productive employment opportunities in India, it is also as a result, a key ingredient in ensuring sustainable poverty reduction. Notwithstanding the efforts made, over the years, at the State and Central levels, through different Programmes, about 40% of the Habitations in the country are still not connected by All-weather roads. It is well known that even where connectivity has been provided, the roads constructed are of such quality (due to poor construction or maintenance) that they cannot always be categorised as All-weather roads.

With a view to redressing the situation, Prime Minister Atal Bihari Vajpayee launched the Pradhan Mantri Gram Sadak Yojana on 25th December, 2000 to provide all-weather access to unconnected habitations. The Pradhan Mantri Gram Sadak Yojana (PMGSY) is a 100% Centrally Sponsored Scheme. 50% of the Cess on High Speed Diesel (HSD) is earmarked for this Yojana.

The Government has brought forward the target date by three years from 2022 to 2019 to achieve complete rural connectivity through all-weather roads under Pradhan Mantri Gram Sadak Yojana (PMGSY). This accelerated implementation will be achieved by providing enhanced financial allocation and through a modified funding pattern in the Scheme. Thus the annual allocation during year 2015-16 is to be enhanced by ₹ 5,000 crore and with this the total Central allocation to States would be ₹ 15,100 crore. 29,000 new habitations will be connected between 2015 to 2017.

Objectives

- The primary objective of the PMGSY is to provide Connectivity, by way of an All-weather Road (with necessary culverts and cross-drainage structures, which is operable throughout the year), to the eligible unconnected Habitations in the rural areas, in such a way that all Unconnected Habitations with a population of 1,000 persons and above are covered in three years (2000-2003) and all Unconnected Habitations with a population of 500 persons and above by the end of the Tenth Plan Period (2007). In respect of the Hill States (North-East, Sikkim, Himachal Pradesh, Jammu & Kashmir, Uttaranchal) and the Desert Areas (as identified in the Desert Development Programme) as well as the Tribal (Schedule V) areas, the objective would be to connect Habitations with a population of 250 persons and above.
- The PMGSY will permit the Upgradation (to prescribed standards) of the existing roads in those Districts where all the eligible Habitations of the designated population size have been provided all-weather road connectivity. However, it must be noted that Upgradation is not central to the Programme and cannot exceed 20% of the State's allocation as long as eligible Unconnected Habitations in the State still exist. In Upgradation

works, priority should be given to Through Routes of the Rural Core Network, which carry more traffic

Guiding Principles of PMGSY and Definitions

1. The spirit and the objective of the Pradhan Mantri Gram Sadak Yojana (PMGSY) is to provide good all-weather road connectivity to unconnected Habitations. A habitation which was earlier provided all-weather connectivity would not be eligible even if the present condition of the road is bad.
2. The unit for this Programme is a Habitation and not a Revenue village or a Panchayat. A Habitation is a cluster of population, living in an area, the location of which does not change over time. Desam, Dhanis, Tolas, Majras, Hamlets etc. are commonly used terminology to describe the Habitations.
3. An Unconnected Habitation is one with a population of designated size located at a distance of at least 500 metres or more (1.5 kms of path distance in case of Hills) from an All-weather road or a connected Habitation.
4. The population, as recorded in the Census 2001, shall be the basis for determining the population size of the Habitation. The population of all Habitations within a radius of 500 metres (1.5 kms of path distance in case of Hills) may be clubbed together for the purpose of determining the population size. This cluster approach would enable provision of connectivity to a larger number of Habitations, particularly in the Hill/ mountainous areas.
5. The eligible Unconnected Habitations are to be connected to nearby Habitations already connected by an All-weather road or to another existing All-weather road so that services (educational, health, marketing facilities etc.), which are not available in the

unconnected Habitation, become available to the residents.

6. A Core Network is that minimal Network of roads (routes) that is essential to provide Basic access to essential social and economic services to all eligible habitations in the selected areas through at least single all-weather road connectivity.
7. A Core Network comprises of Through Routes and Link Routes. Through routes are the ones which collect traffic from several link roads or a long chain of Habitations and lead it to Marketing centres either directly or through the higher category roads ie, the District Roads or the State or National Highway. Link Routes are the roads connecting a single Habitation or a group of Habitations to Through Routes or District Roads leading to Market Centres. Link routes generally have dead ends terminating on a Habitation, while Through Routes arise from the confluence of two or more Link Routes and emerge on to a major Road or to a Market Centre.
8. It should be ensured that each road work that is taken up under the PMGSY is part of the Core Network. While keeping the objective of Connectivity in view, preference should be given to those roads which also incidentally serve other Habitations. In other words, without compromising the basic objective (covering 1,000+ Habitations first and 500+ Habitations next and 250+ Habitations where eligible, last), preference should be given to those roads which serve a larger population. For this purpose, while Habitations within a distance of 500 metres from the road is considered as connected in case of plain areas, this distance should be 1.5 kms (of path length) in respect of Hills.
9. The PMGSY shall cover only the rural areas. Urban roads are excluded from the purview of this Programme. Even in the rural areas, PMGSY covers only

the Rural Roads ie Roads that were formerly classified as 'Other District Roads' (ODR) and 'Village Roads' (VR). Other District Roads (ODR) are roads serving rural areas of production and providing them with outlet to market centres, taluka (tehsil) headquarters, Block headquarters or other main roads. Village Roads (VR) are roads connecting villages/Habitation or groups of Habitation with each other and to the nearest road of a higher category. Major District Roads, State Highways and National Highways cannot be covered under the PMGSY, even if they happen to be in rural areas. This applies to New Connectivity roads as well as Upgradation works.

10. The PMGSY envisages only single road Connectivity to be provided. If a Habitation is already connected by way of an All-weather road, then no new work can be taken up under the PMGSY for that habitation.

11. Provision of connectivity to unconnected Habitations would be termed as New Connectivity. Since the purpose of PMGSY inter alia is to provide farm to market access, new connectivity may involve 'new construction' where the link to the habitation is missing and additionally, if required, 'Upgradation' where an intermediate link in its present condition cannot function as an all-weather road

12. Upgradation, when permitted would typically involve building the base and surface courses of an existing road to desired technical specifications and/or improving the geometrics of the road, as required in accordance with traffic condition.

13. The primary focus of the PMGSY is to provide All-weather road connectivity to the eligible unconnected Habitations. An All-weather road is one which is negotiable in all seasons of the year. This implies that the road-bed is drained effectively (by adequate cross-drainage structures such as culverts, minor bridges and

causeways), but this does not necessarily imply that it should be paved or surfaced or black-topped. Interruptions to traffic as per permitted frequency and duration may be allowed.

14. There may be roads which are Fair-weather roads. In other words, they are fordable only during the dry season, because of lack of Cross Drainage (CD) works. Conversion of such roads to All-weather roads through provision of CD works would be treated as Upgradation. It must be noted that on all the road works of the PMGSY, provision of necessary CD works is considered an essential element
15. PMGSY does not permit repairs to Black-topped or Cement Roads, even if the surface condition is bad.
16. The Rural Roads constructed under the Pradhan Mantri Gram Sadak Yojana will be in accordance with the provision of the Indian Roads Congress (IRC) as given in the Rural Roads Manual (IRC:SP20:2002). In case of Hill Roads, for matters not covered by the Rural Roads Manual, provisions of Hills Roads Manual (IRC:SP:48) may apply.

Planning for Rural Roads

- Proper planning is imperative to achieve the objectives of the Programme in a systematic and cost effective manner. The Manual for the Preparation of District Rural Roads Plan and the Core Network shall be treated as part of the Guidelines and would stand amended to the extent modified by the present Guidelines. The Manual lays down the various steps in the planning process and the role of different Agencies including the Intermediate Panchayat, the District Panchayat as well as the State Level Standing Committee. In the identification of the Core Network, the priorities of elected representatives, including MPs and MLAs, are expected to be duly taken into account and given full consideration. The Rural Roads Plan and the Core Network would constitute the basis for all planning exercises under the PMGSY.

- The District Rural Roads Plan would indicate the entire existing road network system in the District and also clearly identify the proposed roads for providing connectivity to Unconnected Habitations, in an economic and efficient manner in terms of cost and utility. The Core Network will identify the roads required to assure each eligible Habitation with a Basic Access (single all-weather road connectivity) to essential social and economic services. Accordingly, the Core Network would consist of some of the existing roads as well as all the roads proposed for new construction under the PMGSY.
- In proposing the new links under the District Rural Roads Plan, it would be first necessary to indicate the weightage for various services. The District Panchayat shall be the competent authority to select the set of socio-economic/infrastructure variables best suited for the District, categorise them and accord relative weightages to them. This would be communicated to all concerned before commencing the preparation of the District Rural Roads Plan.
- The Plan would first be prepared at the Block level, in accordance with the directions contained in the Manual and the priorities spelt out by the District Panchayat. In short, the existing road network would be drawn up, unconnected Habitations identified and the roads required to connect these unconnected Habitations prepared. This shall constitute the Block Level Master Plan.
- Once this exercise is completed, the Core Network for the Block is identified, by making best use of the existing and proposed road facilities in such a manner that all the eligible Habitations are assured of a Basic

access. It must be ensured that every eligible Habitation is within 500 metres (1.5 kms of Path length in the Hills) of a connected Habitation or an All-weather road (either existing or planned). In drawing up the proposed road links, the requirements of the people must be taken into account, through the socio-economic/infrastructure values (Road Index) suitably weighted and the alignment having the higher Road Index ought to be considered for selection.

- The Block level Master Plan and the Core Network are then placed before the Intermediate Panchayat for consideration and approval of the Core Network. They are simultaneously sent, along with the list of all unconnected Habitations to the Members of Parliament and MLAs, for their comments, if any. After approval by the Intermediate Panchayat, the Plans would be placed before the District Panchayat for its approval. It will be incumbent on the District Panchayat to ensure that the suggestions given by the Members of Parliament are given full consideration within the framework of these Guidelines. Once approved by the District Panchayat, a copy of the Core Network would be sent to the State-level Agency as well as the National Rural Roads Development Agency. No road work may be proposed under the PMGSY for New Connectivity or Upgradation (where permitted) unless it forms part of the Core Network.

Funding and Allocation

Once the Core Network is prepared, it is possible to estimate the length of roads for New Connectivity as well as Upgradation for every District. States may, each year, distribute the State's Allocation among the Districts giving 80% on the basis of road length required for providing connectivity to Unconnected Habitations and 20% on the basis of road length requiring Upgradation under the

PMGSY. The District-wise allocation of funds would also be communicated to the Ministry/NRRDA/and STA every year by the State Government.

In making the District-wise allocation, the road lengths already taken up under the PMGSY or any other Programme may be excluded (even if the road works are still under execution). The figures of new construction length will thus keep on changing every year till such time as all Unconnected Habitations (of the eligible population size) have been covered in the District.

In addition to the allocation to the States, a special allocation of upto 5% of the annual allocation from the Rural Roads share of the Diesel Cess will be made for:

- Districts sharing borders with Pakistan and China (in coordination with Ministry of Home Affairs).
- Districts sharing borders with Myanmar, Bangladesh and Nepal (in coordination with Ministry of Home Affairs).
- Left Wing Extremists areas in the Districts identified by the Ministry of Home Affairs.
- Extremely backward Districts (as identified by the Planning Commission) which can be categorised as Special Problem Areas.
- Research & Development Projects and innovations.

Of 1,78,000 habitations with a population of above 500 in the plains and above 250 in the hilly areas planned to be connected by all-weather roads, 55% (97,838) were connected by March 2014, 82% (80% or 1,31,000 under the PMGSY and 2% or 14,620 under state government schemes) were connected by December 2017. Of the remaining 47,000, work on all is in progress except for 1,700 which will be approved by the end of December 2017 and 100% connectivity will be achieved by March 2019 (16 December 2017 update). Pending work included harsh terrain states of

Assam, Jammu and Kashmir and Uttarakhand as well as left-wing Naxalite-Maoist extremism infested state of Chhattisgarh, some districts of Jharkhand and Malkangiri district of Odisha.

The average speed of road construction under the PMGSY was 98.5 kms per day from 2004 to 2014, it rose to 130 kms per day in 2016-17. On date it has been able to cover more than 80% of its original target. Scheme has started to change the lifestyle of many villagers with new roads and upgrades, such as in Manipur.

5

Lahore Summit

Lahore Declaration was a bilateral agreement and governance treaty between India and Pakistan. The treaty was signed on 21 February 1999, at the conclusion of a historic summit in Lahore, and ratified by the parliaments of both countries the same year.

Under the terms of the treaty, a mutual understanding was reached towards the development of atomic arsenals and to avoid accidental and unauthorised operational use of nuclear weapons. The Lahore Declaration brought added responsibility to both nations' leadership towards avoiding nuclear race, as well as both non-conventional and conventional conflicts. This event was significant in the history of Pakistan and it provided both countries an environment of mutual confidence. In a much-covered televised press conference in both countries, Prime Minister Nawaz Sharif and Prime Minister Atal Bihari Vajpayee signed the treaty. It was the second nuclear control treaty signed by both countries and pledged to continue the use of the first treaty, NNAA, was signed in 1988. The Lahore treaty was quickly ratified by the parliaments of India and Pakistan and came into force the same year.

The Lahore Declaration signalled a major breakthrough in overcoming the historically strained bilateral relations between the two nations in the aftermath of the publicly performed atomic tests carried out by both nations in May 1998. Widely popular in the public circles in Pakistan and hailed by the international community, the relations would soon lose impetus with the outbreak of the controversial Kargil debacle in May 1999.

The Lahore treaty was one of the most important and historical treaties of India and Pakistan to normalise the relations to ease up the military tensions in South Asia. In 1972, the Shimla Treaty was acceded to establish peaceful relations in the aftermath of the disastrous war in 1971 and committed both nations to resolving bilateral disputes by peaceful dialogue and co-operation. In 1978, Pakistan made a proposal to limit the nuclear race between two countries and to establish South Asia Nuclear Weapon Free Zone (SANWFZ), for which negotiations were never concluded.

In 1988, Pakistan and India reached an important understanding towards controlling the nuclear weapons, and signed the NNAA treaty. Despite many proposals, the nuclear race continued and the cold war had been heightened over the issue of Kashmir. The domestic pressure and the increasingly political momentum, India conducted the nuclear tests on May 1998, in spite of international pressure. Responding to India's test, Pakistan equalised the nuclear magnitude in South Asia after performing its own series of atomic tests, all in the end month of May 1998. The tests invited condemnation and economic sanctions on both countries and many fear in the international community that in a wake of intensified conflict, it could lead to nuclear war.

Negotiations

In 1998, the Foreign ministries of both countries had been initiating peace process to ease up the tension in the region. On 23 September 1998 both governments signed an agreement recognising the principle of building an environment of peace and security and resolving all bilateral conflicts, which became the basis of the Lahore Declaration. On 11 February 1999, the Pakistan Foreign Office announced the state visit of Indian Prime minister Atal Bihari Vajpayee aboard the maiden bus service between the two countries.

Before the arrival of Indian Prime Minister, a warm welcome awaited Indian Prime Minister Vajpayee when he arrived at Wagah by the inaugural bus service between New Delhi and Lahore. He was received by Prime Minister Nawaz Sharif and the units of Pakistan Army gave the Indian Prime minister a guard of honour. It embarked on a historic visit to Pakistan, travelling on the inaugural bus service connecting the Indian capital of New Delhi with the major Pakistani city of Lahore, establishing a major transport link for the peoples of both nations. The inaugural bus also carried Indian celebrities and dignitaries such as Dev Anand, Satish Gujral, Javed Akhtar, Kuldip Nayar, Kapil Dev, Shatrughan Sinha and Mallika Sarabhai. He was received amidst great fanfare and media attention at the Pakistani border post of Wagah by Pakistan Prime minister Nawaz Sharif, with whom he had been at loggerheads a year before over the nuclear tests controversy. The summit was hailed worldwide as a major breakthrough and milestone in bilateral relations and a historic step towards ending conflict and tensions in the region.

Drafting and Signatures

The Lahore Declaration is one notable treaty after the 1988 NNAA treaty and the 1972 Shimla Treaty. After the two Prime ministers signed the agreement, the foreign secretaries of Pakistan Shamshad Ahmad and India K Raghunath signed an MoU on 21 February 1999, identifying measures aimed at promoting an environment of peace and security between the two countries. The MoU reaffirmed the continued commitment of their respective governments to the principles and purposes of the UN Charter.

The MoU reiterated the determination of both countries to implementing the Simla Agreement in letter and spirit; and that an environment of peace and security is in the national interest of both countries and that resolution of all outstanding issues, including Jammu and Kashmir, is essential for this purpose. The parliaments of both countries quickly ratified and acceded the treaties following the signatures.

The Lahore Declaration was signed on 21 February along with a memorandum of understanding (MoU) after three rounds of talks between the Indian and Pakistani leaders. In its content, both governments asserted their commitment to the vision of peace, stability and mutual progress and their full commitment to the Simla Agreement and the UN Charter. Both governments recognised through the Lahore Declaration that the development of nuclear weapons brought added responsibility to both nations towards avoiding conflict and promoted the importance of Confidence-building measures, especially to avoid accidental and unauthorised use of nuclear weapons. India and Pakistan also decided to give each other advance notification of ballistic missile flight tests and accidental or unexplained use of nuclear weapons to avoid the outbreak of a nuclear conflict. Its important inter alia stated:

- Recognizes that the nuclear dimension of the security environment of the two countries adds to their responsibility for avoidance of conflict between them.
- Commits both to the principles and purposes of the Charter of the United Nations, and the universally accepted principles of peaceful co-existence.
- Commits both countries to the objectives of universal nuclear disarmament and nonproliferation.

The Lahore Declaration and the MoU incorporated a joint commitment to intensify efforts to resolve the Kashmir conflict and other dispute, to enhance bilateral dialogue and to implement nuclear safeguards and measures to prevent conflict. Both governments condemned terrorism and committed to non-interference in each other's internal affairs and the objectives of the South Asia Association for Regional Cooperation and promote human rights.

In the joint statement issued after the conclusion of the summit, both governments said that their foreign ministers would meet periodically and consult each other on issues pertaining to the World Trade Organization and information technology. A two-member ministerial committee was to be established to investigate human rights issues, civilian detainees and missing prisoners of war. The Indian Prime Minister thanked his Pakistani counterpart and issued an invitation for a future summit in India.

The Lahore Declaration was hailed warmly in India and in the global media and by governments of other nations, forging optimism after the global tensions over the 1998 nuclear tests. The initiative bolstered the popularity of the Vajpayee government in India, cementing his standing as a statesman.

Relations between the two nations were completely transformed at the outbreak of the Kargil War in May 1999, following the sudden revelation that Pakistani soldiers had infiltrated into Indian Kashmir; the Indian Army was deployed to evict the Pakistan army soldiers and retake capture the disputed territory. The two-month-long conflict claimed the lives of hundreds of soldiers on both sides and brought both nations close to full-scale war and possible nuclear conflict. After this conflict, the "Lahore Treaty" was stalled and no further discussions took place between the two countries on promoting the dialogue and CBMs initiated at Lahore in February 1999.

The conflict was followed by an Atlantique incident in which the Indian Air Force intercept and shot down the Pakistan Navy's reconnaissance aircraft; a total of eleven naval personnel were killed. After months of contentious relations with the military and judiciary, a military coup d'état was staged by Pakistan Armed Forces that overthrew the government of Nawaz Sharif and brought the chairman joint chiefs General Pervez Musharraf, believed to be responsible for the Kargil incursion, to power, thus exacerbating doubts over the future of the relations between the two nations. Despite many political difficulties, India reiterated the necessity of implementing the Simla and Lahore treaties and said India would support the Simla Agreement, Lahore Declaration, and the issue of cross-border terrorism.

6

Kargil War

Kargil War was an armed conflict between India and Pakistan that took place between May and July 1999 in the Kargil district of Kashmir and elsewhere along the Line of Control (LoC). Kargil War is also referred to as Operation Vijay which was the name of the Indian operation to clear the Kargil sector.

The cause of the war was the infiltration of Pakistani soldiers disguised as Kashmiri militants into positions on the Indian side of the LoC, which serves as the *de facto* border between the two states. During the initial stages of the war, Pakistan blamed the fighting entirely on independent Kashmiri insurgents, but documents left behind by casualties and later statements by Pakistan's Prime Minister and Chief of Army Staff showed involvement of Pakistani paramilitary forces, led by General Ashraf Rashid. The Indian Army, later supported by the Indian Air Force, recaptured the positions on the Indian side of the LoC infiltrated by the Pakistani troops and militants. Facing international diplomatic opposition, Pakistani forces withdrew from the remaining Indian positions along the LoC.

The war is one of the most recent examples of high-altitude warfare in mountainous terrain, which posed significant logistical problems for the combating sides. It is also one of the very few instances of direct, conventional warfare between nuclear states (ie those possessing nuclear weapons). India had conducted its first successful test in 1974; Pakistan, which had been developing its nuclear capability in secret since around the same time, conducted its first known tests in 1998, just two weeks after a second series of tests by India.

Before the Partition of India in 1947, Kargil was part of the Baltistan district of Ladakh, a sparsely populated region with diverse linguistic, ethnic and religious groups, living in isolated valleys separated by some of the world's highest mountains. The First Kashmir War (1947-48) concluded with the LoC bisecting the Baltistan district, with the town and district of Kargil lying on the Indian side in the Ladakh subdivision of the Indian State of Jammu and Kashmir. After Pakistan's defeat in the Indo-Pakistani War of 1971, the two nations signed the Simla Agreement promising not to engage in armed conflict with respect to that boundary.

The town of Kargil is located 205 kms from Srinagar, facing the Northern Areas across the LoC. Like other areas in the Himalayas, Kargil has a continental climate. Summers are cool with frigid nights, while winters are long and chilly with temperatures often dropping to –48°C (–54°F).

National Highway (NH 1D) connecting Srinagar to Leh cuts through Kargil. The area that witnessed the infiltration and fighting is a 160 kms long stretch of ridges overlooking this only road linking Srinagar and Leh. The military outposts on the ridges above the highway were generally around 5,000 metres (16,000 ft) high, with a few as high as 5,485 metres (18,000 ft). Apart from the district capital, Kargil, the populated areas near the front line in the conflict included the Mushko Valley and the town of Drass, southwest of Kargil, as well as the Batalik sector and other areas, northeast of Kargil.

Kargil was targeted partly because the terrain was conducive to the pre-emptive seizure of several unoccupied military positions. With tactically vital features and well-prepared defensive posts atop the peaks, a defender on the high ground would enjoy advantages akin to a fortress. Any attack to dislodge a defender from high ground in mountain warfare requires a far higher ratio of attackers to defenders, and the difficulties would be exacerbated by the high altitude and freezing temperatures.

Kargil is just 173 kms from the Pakistani-controlled town of Skardu, which was capable of providing logistical and artillery support to Pakistani combatants. A road between Kargil and Skardu exists, which was closed in 1949.

After the Indo-Pakistan War of 1971, there had been a long period with relatively few direct armed conflicts involving the military forces of the two neighbours - notwithstanding the efforts of both nations to control the Siachen Glacier by establishing military outposts on the surrounding mountains ridges and the resulting military skirmishes in the 1980s. During the 1990s, however, escalating tensions and conflict due to separatist activities in Kashmir, some of which were supported by Pakistan, as well as the conducting of nuclear tests by both countries in 1998, led to an increasingly belligerent atmosphere. In an attempt to defuse the situation, both countries signed the Lahore Declaration in February 1999, promising to provide a peaceful and bilateral solution to the Kashmir conflict.

During the winter of 1998-1999, some elements of the Pakistani Armed Forces were covertly training and sending Pakistani troops and paramilitary forces, some allegedly in the guise of Mujahideen, into territory on the Indian side of the LoC. The infiltration was codenamed Operation Badr; its aim was to sever the link between Kashmir and Ladakh, and cause Indian forces to withdraw from the Siachen Glacier, thus forcing India to negotiate a settlement of the broader Kashmir dispute. Pakistan also believed that any tension in the region would internationalise the Kashmir issue, helping it to secure a speedy resolution. Yet another goal may have been to boost the morale of the decade-long rebellion in Indian Administered Kashmir by taking a pro-active role.

Pakistani Lieutenant General Shahid Aziz, and then head of ISI analysis wing, has confirmed there were no Mujahideen but only regular Pakistan Army soldiers who took part in the Kargil War. "There were no Mujahideen, only taped wireless messages, which fooled no one. Our soldiers were made to occupy barren ridges, with hand held weapons and ammunition", Lt Gen Aziz wrote in his article in *The Nation* daily in January 2013.

Some writers have speculated that the operation's objective may also have been retaliation for India's Operation Meghdoot in 1984 that seized much of Siachen Glacier.

According to India's then Army Chief Ved Prakash Malik, and many scholars, much of the background planning, including construction of logistical supply routes, had been undertaken much earlier. On several occasions during the 1980s and 1990s, the army had given Pakistani leaders (Zia ul Haq and Benazir Bhutto) similar proposals for infiltration into the Kargil region, but the plans had been shelved for fear of drawing the nations into all-out war.

Some analysts believe that the blueprint of attack was reactivated soon after Pervez Musharraf was appointed Chief of Army Staff in October 1998. After the war, Nawaz Sharif, Prime Minister of Pakistan during the Kargil conflict, claimed that he was unaware of the plans, and that he first learned about the situation when he received an urgent phone call from Atal Bihari Vajpayee, his counterpart in India. Sharif attributed the plan to Musharraf and "just two or three of his cronies", a view shared by some Pakistani writers who have stated that only four generals, including Musharraf, knew of the plan. Musharraf, however, asserted that Sharif had been briefed on the Kargil operation 15 days ahead of Vajpayee's journey to Lahore on 20 February.

Conflict Events

3 May	Pakistani intrusion in Kargil reported by local shepherds.
5 May	Indian Army patrol sent up; five Indian soldiers captured and tortured to death.
9 May	Heavy shelling by Pakistan Army damages ammunition dump in Kargil.
10 May	Infiltrations first noticed in Dras, Kaksar, and Mushkoh sectors.
Mid-May	Indian Army moves in more troops from Kashmir Valley to Kargil Sector.
26 May	IAF launches air strikes against infiltrators.
27 May	IAF loses two fighters - MiG-21 and MiG-27; Flt Lt Nachiketa taken PoW.
28 May	IAF MI-17 shot down by Pakistan; four air crew dead.
1 June	Pakistan steps up attacks; bombs NH 1A.
5 June	Indian Army releases documents recovered from three Pakistani soldiers indicating Pakistan's involvement.
6 June	Indian Army launches major offensive in Kargil.
9 June	Indian Army re-captures two key positions in the Batalic sector.
11 June	India releases intercepts of conversation between Pakistani Army Chief Gen Pervez Musharraf, while on a visit to China and Chief of General Staff Lt Gen Aziz Khan in Rawalpindi, as proof of Pakistani Army's involvement.
13 June	Indian Army secures Tololing in Dras.
15 June	US President Bill Clinton, in a telephonic conversation, asks Pakistani Prime Minister Nawaz Sharif to pull out from Kargil.
29 June	Indian Army captures two vital posts: Point 5060 and Point 5100 near Tiger Hill.

2 July	Indian Army launches three-pronged attack in Kargil.
4 July	Indian Army recaptures Tiger Hill after an 11-hour battle.
5 July	Indian Army takes control of Dras. Sharif announces Pakistani army's withdrawal from Kargil following his meeting with Clinton.
7 July	India recaptures Jubar Heights in Batalik.
11 July	Pakistan begins pullout; India captures key peaks in Batalik.
14 July	Indian Prime Minister Atal Bihari Vajpayee declares Operation Vijay a success. Government sets condition for talks with Pakistan.
26 July	Kargil conflict officially comes to an end. Indian Army announces complete eviction of Pakistani intruders.

There were three major phases to the Kargil War. First, Pakistan infiltrated forces into the Indian-controlled section of Kashmir and occupied strategic locations enabling it to bring NH1 within range of its artillery fire. The next stage consisted of India discovering the infiltration and mobilising forces to respond to it. The final stage involved major battles by Indian and Pakistani forces resulting in India recapturing most of the territories held by Pakistani forces and the subsequent withdrawal of Pakistani forces back across the Line of Control after international pressure.

Occupation by Pakistan

During February 1999, the Pakistan Army sent forces to occupy some posts on the Indian side of the LoC. Troops from the elite Special Services Group as well as four to seven battalions of the Northern Light Infantry (a paramilitary regiment not part of the regular Pakistani army at that time) covertly and overtly set up bases on the vantage points of the Indian-controlled region. According to some reports, these Pakistani forces were backed by Kashmiri guerrillas and Afghan mercenaries. According to General Ved Malik, the bulk of the infiltration occurred in April 1999.

Pakistani intrusions took place in the heights of the lower Mushkoh Valley, along the Marpo La ridgeline in Dras, in Kaksar near Kargil, in the Batalik sector east of the Indus River, on the heights above of the Chorbatla sector where the LoC turns North and in the Turtok sector south of the Siachen area.

India Discovers Infiltration

Initially, these incursions were not detected for a number of reasons: Indian patrols were not sent into some of the areas infiltrated by the Pakistani forces and heavy artillery fire by Pakistan in some areas provided cover for the infiltrators. But by the second week of May, the ambushing of an Indian patrol team led by Capt Saurabh Kalia, who acted on a tip-off by a local shepherd in the Batalik sector, led to the exposure of the infiltration. Initially, with little knowledge of the nature or extent of the infiltration, the Indian troops in the area assumed that the infiltrators were jihadis and claimed that they would evict them within a few days. Subsequent discovery of infiltration elsewhere along the LoC, and the difference in tactics employed by the infiltrators, caused the Indian army to realise that the plan of attack was on a much bigger scale. The total area seized by the ingress is generally accepted to between 130-200 km^2.

Government of India responded with Operation Vijay, a mobilisation of 2,00,000 Indian troops. However, because of the nature of the terrain, division and corps operations could not be mounted; subsequent fighting was conducted mostly at the regimental or battalion level. In effect, two divisions of the Indian Army, numbering 20,000, plus several thousand from the Paramilitary forces of India and the air force were deployed in the conflict zone. The total number of Indian soldiers that were involved in the military operation on the Kargil-Drass sector was thus close to 30,000. The number of infiltrators, including those providing logistical backup, has been put at approximately 5,000 at the height of the conflict. This figure includes troops from Pakistan-Occupied Kashmir who provided additional artillery support.

The Indian Air Force launched Operation Safed Sagar in support of the mobilisation of Indian land forces, but its effectiveness during the war was limited by the high altitude and weather conditions, which in turn limited bomb loads and the number of airstrips that could be used.

Naval Action

The Indian Navy also prepared to blockade the Pakistani ports (primarily the Karachi port) to cut off supply routes under Operation Talwar. The Indian Navy's western and eastern fleets joined in the North Arabian Sea and began aggressive patrols and threatened to cut Pakistan's sea trade. This exploited Pakistan's dependence on sea-based oil and trade flows. Later, then-Prime Minister of Pakistan, Nawaz Sharif disclosed that Pakistan was left with just six days of fuel to sustain itself if a full-scale war had broken out.

India Attacks Pakistani Positions

The terrain of Kashmir is mountainous and at high altitudes; even the best roads, such as National Highway 1D from Leh to Srinagar, are only two lanes. The rough terrain and narrow roads slowed down traffic, and the high altitude, which affected the ability of aircraft to carry loads, made control of NH 1D (the actual stretch of the highway which was under Pakistani fire) a priority for India. From their observation posts, the Pakistani forces had a clear line-of-sight to lay down indirect artillery fire on NH 1D, inflicting heavy casualties on the Indians. This was a serious problem for the Indian Army as the highway was the main logistical and supply route. The Pakistani shelling of the arterial road posed the threat of Leh being cut off, though an alternative (and longer) road to Leh existed via Himachal Pradesh.

The infiltrators, apart from being equipped with small arms and grenade launchers, were also armed with mortars, artillery and anti-aircraft guns. Many posts were also heavily mined, with India later stating to have recovered more than 8,000 anti-personnel mines according to an ICBL report. Pakistan's reconnaissance was done through unmanned aerial vehicles and AN/TPQ-36 Firefinder radars supplied by the US. The initial Indian attacks were aimed at controlling the hills overlooking NH 1D, with high priority being given to the stretches of the highway near the town of Kargil. The majority of posts along the Line of Control were adjacent to the highway, and therefore the recapture of nearly every infiltrated post increased both the territorial gains and the security of the highway. The protection of this route and the recapture of the forward posts were thus ongoing objectives throughout the war.

Indian Army's first priority was to recapture peaks that were in the immediate vicinity of NH 1D. This resulted in Indian troops first targeting the Tiger Hill and Tololing complex in Dras, which dominated the Srinagar-Leh route. This was soon followed by the Batalik-Turtok sub-sector which provided access to Siachen Glacier. Some of the peaks that were of vital strategic importance to the Pakistani defensive troops were Point 4590 and Point 5353. While 4590 was the nearest point that had a view of NH 1D, point 5353 was the highest feature in the Dras sector, allowing the Pakistani troops to observe NH 1D. The recapture of Point 4590 by Indian troops on 14 June was significant, notwithstanding the fact that it resulted in the Indian Army suffering the most casualties in a single battle during the conflict. Though most of the posts in the vicinity of the highway were cleared by mid-June, some parts of the highway near Drass witnessed sporadic shelling until the end of the war.

Once India regained control of the hills overlooking NH 1D, the Indian Army turned to driving the invading force back across the Line of Control. The Battle of Tololing, amongst other assaults, slowly tilted the combat in India's favour. The Pakistani troops at Tololing were aided by Pakistani fighters from Kashmir. Some of the posts put up a stiff resistance, including Tiger Hill (Point 5140) that fell only later in the war. Indian troops found well-entrenched Pakistani soldiers at Tiger Hill, and both sides suffered heavy casualties. After a final assault on the peak in which ten Pakistani soldiers and five Indian soldiers were killed, Tiger Hill finally fell. A few of the assaults occurred atop hitherto unheard of peaks - most of them unnamed with only Point numbers to differentiate them - which witnessed fierce hand to hand combat.

As the operation was fully underway, about 250 artillery guns were brought in to clear the infiltrators in the posts that were in the line-of-sight. The Bofors FH-77B field howitzer played a vital role, with Indian gunners making maximum use of the terrain. However, its success was limited elsewhere due to the lack of space and depth to deploy it.

It was in this type of terrain that aerial attacks were used with limited effectiveness. French made Mirage 2000H of the IAF were tasked to drop laser-guided bombs to destroy well-entrenched positions of the Pakistani forces. The IAF lost a MiG-27 strike aircraft, which it attributed to an engine failure, and a MiG-21 fighter which was shot down by Pakistan; initially Pakistan said it shot down both jets after they crossed into its territory. One Indian Mi-8 helicopter was also lost due to Stinger SAMs. On 27 May 1999, Flt Lt Nachiketa developed engine trouble in the Batalik sector and bailed out of his craft. Sqn Ldr Ajay Ahuja went out of his way to locate his comrade but was shot down by a shoulder-fired Stinger missile. According to reports, he had bailed out of his stricken plane safely but was apparently killed by his captors as his body was returned riddled with bullet wounds.

In many vital points, neither artillery nor air power could dislodge the outposts manned by the Pakistani soldiers, who were out of visible range. The Indian Army mounted some direct frontal ground assaults which were slow and took a heavy toll given the steep ascent that had to be made on peaks as high as 18,000 feet (5,500 m). Since any daylight attack would be suicidal, all the advances had to be made under the cover of darkness, escalating the risk of freezing. Accounting for the wind chill factor, the temperatures were often as low as –15°C to –11°C (12°F to 5°F) near the mountain tops. Based on military tactics, much of the costly frontal assaults by the Indians could have been avoided if the Indian Military had chosen to blockade the supply route of the opposing force, creating a siege. Such a move would have involved the Indian troops crossing the LoC as well as initiating aerial attacks on Pakistani soil, a manoeuvre India was not willing to exercise fearing an expansion of the theatre of war and reduced international support for its cause.

Two months into the conflict, Indian troops had slowly retaken most of the ridges that were encroached by the infiltrators; according to the official count, an estimated 75–80% of the intruded area and nearly all the high ground were back under Indian control.

Withdrawal and Final Battles

Following the outbreak of armed fighting, Pakistan sought American help in de-escalating the conflict. Bruce Riedel, who was then an aide to President Bill Clinton, reported that US intelligence had imaged Pakistani movements of nuclear weapons to forward deployments for fear of the Kargil hostilities escalating into a wider conflict. However,

President Clinton refused to intervene until Pakistan had removed all forces from the Indian side of the Line of Control. Following the Washington accord of 4 July 1999, when Sharif agreed to withdraw Pakistani troops, most of the fighting came to a gradual halt, but some Pakistani forces remained in positions on the Indian side of the LoC. In addition, the United Jihad Council (an umbrella for extremist groups) rejected Pakistan's plan for a climb-down, instead deciding to fight on.

The Indian army launched its final attacks in the last week of July; as soon as the Drass subsector had been cleared of Pakistani forces, the fighting ceased on 26 July. The day has since been marked as Kargil Vijay Diwas (Kargil Victory Day) celebrated annually in India. By the end of the war, Pakistan had to withdraw under international pressure and due to pressure from continued fighting at battle front and left India in control of all territory south and east of the Line of Control, as was established in July 1972 as per the Simla Agreement.

Pakistan was criticised by many countries for instigating the war, as its paramilitary forces and insurgents crossed the Line of Control. Pakistan's primary diplomatic response, one of plausible deniability linking the incursion to what it officially termed as 'Kashmiri freedom fighters', was in the end not successful. Veteran analysts argued that the battle was fought at heights where only seasoned troops could survive, so poorly equipped 'freedom fighters' would neither have the ability nor the wherewithal to seize land and defend it. Moreover, while the army had initially denied the involvement of its troops in the intrusion, two soldiers were awarded the Nishan-e-Haider (Pakistan's highest military honour). Another 90 soldiers were also given gallantry awards, most of them posthumously, confirming Pakistan's role in the episode. India also released taped phone conversations between the Army Chief and a senior Pakistani General where the latter is recorded saying: "the scruff of [the militants] necks is in our hands," although

Pakistan dismissed it as a 'total fabrication'. Concurrently, Pakistan made several contradicting statements, confirming its role in Kargil, when it defended the incursions saying that the LoC itself was disputed. Pakistan also attempted to internationalise the Kashmir issue, by linking the crisis in Kargil to the larger Kashmir conflict but, such a diplomatic stance found few backers on the world stage.

As the Indian counter-attacks picked up momentum, Pakistani Prime Minister Nawaz Sharif flew to meet US President Bill Clinton on 4 July to obtain support from the United States. Clinton rebuked Sharif, however, and asked him to use his contacts to rein in the militants and withdraw Pakistani soldiers from Indian territory. Clinton would later reveal in his autobiography that "Sharif's moves were perplexing" since the Indian Prime Minister had travelled to Lahore to promote bilateral talks aimed at resolving the Kashmir problem and "by crossing the Line of Control, Pakistan had wrecked the [bilateral] talks." On the other hand, he applauded Indian restraint for not crossing the LoC and escalating the conflict into an all-out war.

G8 nations supported India and condemned Pakistani violation of the LoC at the Cologne Summit. The European Union also opposed Pakistan's violation of the LoC. China, a long-time ally of Pakistan, insisted on a pullout of forces to the pre-conflict positions along the LoC and settling border issues peacefully. Other organisations like the ASEAN Regional Forum too supported India's stand on the inviolability of the LoC.

Faced with growing international pressure, Sharif managed to pull back the remaining soldiers from Indian territory. The joint statement issued by Clinton and Sharif conveyed the need to respect the Line of Control and resume bilateral talks as the best forum to resolve all disputes.

Gallantry Awards

A number of Indian soldiers earned awards for gallantry:

- Grenadier Yogendra Singh Yadav, 18 Grenadiers, Param Vir Chakra
- Lieutenant Manoj Kumar Pandey, 1/11 Gorkha Rifles, Param Vir Chakra, Posthumous
- Captain Vikram Batra, 13 JAK Rifles, Param Vir Chakra, Posthumous
- Rifleman Sanjay Kumar, 13 JAK Rifles, Param Vir Chakra
- Captain Anuj Nayyar, 17 JAT Regiment, Maha Vir Chakra, Posthumous
- Major Rajesh Singh Adhikari, 18 Grenadiers, Maha Vir Chakra, Posthumous
- Captain Haneef-ud-din, 11 Rajputana Rifles, Vir Chakra, posthumous
- Major Mariappan Saravanan, 1 Bihar, Vir Chakra, Posthumous
- Squadron Leader Ajay Ahuja, Indian Air Force, Vir Chakra, Posthumous
- Havildar Chuni Lal, 8 JAK LI, Vir Chakra. Also awarded Sena Medal for gallantry and posthumously awarded Ashoka Chakra as a Naib Subedar.
- Colonel Magod Basappa Ravindranath, 2 Rajputana Rifles, Vir Chakra

Since Pakistan and India each had weapons of mass destruction, many in the international community were concerned that if the Kargil conflict intensified, it could lead to nuclear war. Both countries had tested their nuclear capability in 1998 (India conducted its first test in 1974 while it was Pakistan's first-ever nuclear test). Many pundits believed the tests to be an indication of the escalating stakes in the scenario in South Asia. When the Kargil conflict started just a year after the nuclear tests, many nations desired to end it before it intensified.

International concerns increased when Pakistani Foreign Secretary Shamshad Ahmad made a statement on 31 May warning that an escalation of the limited conflict could lead Pakistan to use 'any weapon' in its arsenal. This was immediately interpreted as a threat of nuclear retaliation by Pakistan in the event of an extended war, and the belief was reinforced when the leader of Pakistan's senate noted, "The purpose of developing weapons becomes meaningless if they are not used when they are needed." Many such ambiguous statements from officials of both countries were viewed as warnings of an impending nuclear crisis where the combatants would consider use of their limited nuclear arsenals in 'tactical' nuclear warfare in the belief that it would not have ended in mutual assured destruction, as could have occurred in a nuclear conflict between the United States and the USSR. Some experts believe that following nuclear tests in 1998, the Pakistani military was emboldened by its nuclear deterrent to markedly increase coercion against India.

The nature of the India-Pakistan conflict took a more sinister turn when the United States received intelligence that Pakistani nuclear warheads were being moved towards the border. Bill Clinton tried to dissuade Pakistan Prime Minister Nawaz Sharif from nuclear brinkmanship, even threatening Pakistan of dire consequences. According to a White House official, Sharif seemed to be genuinely surprised by this supposed missile movement and responded that India was probably planning the same.

Sensing a deteriorating military scenario, diplomatic isolation, and the risks of a larger conventional and nuclear war, Sharif ordered the Pakistani army to vacate the Kargil heights. He later claimed in his official biography that General Pervez Musharraf had moved nuclear warheads without informing him. Recently however, Pervez Musharraf revealed in his memoirs that Pakistan's nuclear delivery system was not operational during the Kargil war; something that would have put Pakistan under serious disadvantage if the conflict went nuclear.

The threat of WMD included chemical and even biological weapons. Pakistan accused India of using chemical weapons and incendiary weapons such as napalm against the Kashmiri fighters. India, on the other hand, showcased a cache of gas masks as proof that Pakistan may have been prepared to use non-conventional weapons. US official and the Organisation for the Prohibition of Chemical Weapons determined that Pakistani allegations of India using banned chemicals in its bombs were unfounded.

From the end of the war until February 2000, the Indian stock market rose by more than 30%. The next Indian national budget included major increases in military spending.

There was a surge in patriotism, with many celebrities expressing their support for the Kargil cause. Indians were angered by media reports of the death of pilot Ajay Ahuja, especially after Indian authorities reported that Ahuja had been murdered and his body mutilated by Pakistani troops. The war had produced higher than expected fatalities for the Indian military, with a sizeable percentage of them including newly commissioned officers. One month after conclusion of the Kargil War, the Atlantique Incident, in which a Pakistan Navy plane was shot down by India, briefly re-ignited fears of a conflict between the two countries.

After the war, the Indian government severed ties with Pakistan and increased defence preparedness. India increased its defence budget as it sought to acquire more state of the art equipment. Media reported about military procurement irregularities and criticism of intelligence agencies like Research and Analysis Wing, which failed to predict the intrusions or the identity/number of infiltrators during the war. An internal assessment report by the armed forces, published in an Indian magazine, showed several other failings, including "a sense of complacency" and being "unprepared for a conventional war" on the presumption that nuclearism would sustain peace. It also highlighted the lapses in command and control, the insufficient troop levels and the dearth of large-calibre guns like the Bofors. In 2006, retired Air Chief Marshal AY Tipnis, alleged that the Indian Army did not fully inform the government about the intrusions, adding that the Army Chief Ved Prakash Malik, was initially reluctant to use the full strike capability of the Indian Air Force, instead requesting only helicopter gunship support. Soon after the conflict, India also decided to complete the project, previously stalled by Pakistan, to fence the entire LoC.

Kargil Review Committee

Soon after the war the Atal Bihari Vajpayee government set up an inquiry into its causes and to analyse perceived Indian intelligence failures. The high-powered committee was chaired by eminent strategic affairs analyst K Subrahmanyam and given powers to interview anyone with current or past associations with Indian security, including former Prime Ministers. The committee's final report (also referred to as the 'Subrahmanyam Report') led to a large-scale restructuring of Indian Intelligence. It, however, came in for heavy criticism in the Indian media for its perceived avoidance of assigning specific responsibility for failures over detecting the Kargil intrusions. The Committee was also embroiled in controversy for indicting Brigadier Surinder Singh of the Indian Army for his failure to report enemy intrusions in time, and for his subsequent conduct. Many press reports questioned or contradicted this finding and claimed that Singh had in fact issued early warnings that were ignored by senior Indian Army commanders and, ultimately, higher government functionaries.

Kargil War Memorial

Kargil War memorial, built by the Indian Army, is located in Dras, in the foothills of the Tololing Hill. The memorial, located about 5 km from the city centre across the Tiger Hill, commemorates the martyrs of the Kargil War. The names of the soldiers who lost their lives in the War are inscribed on the Memorial Wall. A museum attached to the Kargil War Memorial, which was established to celebrate the victory of 'Operation Vijay', houses pictures of Indian soldiers, archives of important war documents and recordings, Pakistani war equipments and gear, and official emblems of the Army from the Kargil War.

7

Parliament Attack

Parliament attack in 2001 was a terrorist attack at the Parliament of India in New Delhi on 13 December 2001. Lashkar-e-Taiba (LeT) and Jaish-e-Mohammed (JeM) - two terrorist organizations were involved in the attack. The attack on the symbol of Indian democracy led to the death of 6 Delhi Police personnel, 2 Parliament Security Service personnel, a gardener and 5 terrorists, to increased tensions between India and Pakistan, resulting in the 2001–02 India-Pakistan standoff.

On 13th December 2001, five terrorists infiltrated the Parliament House in a car with Home Ministry and Parliament labels. While both the Rajya Sabha and Lok Sabha had been adjourned 40 minutes prior to the incident, many Members of Parliament (MPs) and government officials such as Home Minister LK Advani and Minister of State for Defence Harin Pathak were believed to have still been in the building at the time of the attack. More than 100 people, including major politicians were inside the Parliament building at the time. The gunmen used a fake identity sticker on the car they drove and thus breached the security deployed around the Parliamentary complex. The terrorists carried AK47 rifles, grenade launchers, pistols and grenades.

The gunmen drove their vehicle into the car of the Vice-President Krishan Kant, got out, and began shooting. The Vice-President's guards and security personnel shot back at the terrorists and then started closing the gates of the compound. A similar attack was carried out on the assembly of Jammu and Kashmir (Srinagar), during November 2001, when 38 people were killed by terrorists.

CRPF Constable Kamlesh Kumari was the first to spot the terrorists and was shot by them as she raised the alarm. She died on the spot. One gunman's suicide vest exploded when he was shot dead; the other 4 gunmen were also killed. Five policemen, a Parliament security guard, and a gardener were killed and 18 others were injured. The ministers and MPs escaped unhurt. Total number of deaths was 14 and at least 22 people were injured in the attack. Delhi Police claimed that gunmen received instructions from Pakistan and the operation was carried out under the guidance of Pakistan's Inter-Services Intelligence (ISI).

Following the attack, many suspects were arrested, and in December 2002 four Jaish-e-Mohammed members were convicted for roles in the attack. In 2003, the Border Security Force (BSF) killed Ghazi Baba, the Commander-in-Chief of Jaish-e-Mohammed and the mastermind of the attack.

World leaders condemned the attack on the Parliament. On 14 December, the ruling National Democratic Alliance (NDA) blamed Pakistan-based Lashkar-e-Taiba and Jaish-e-Mohammed for the attack. Home Minister LK Advani claimed, "We have received some clues about yesterday's incident, which shows that a neighbouring country, and some terrorist organisations active there behind it," in an indirect reference to Pakistan and Pakistan-based terrorist groups.

Special Court Judgement

Special Judge SN Dhingra convicted three of the four accused, in the case relating to the 13th December 2001 attack on Parliament House, for waging a war against the State. These persons were Mohammed Afzal, Shaukat Hussain Guru and Syed Abdul Rehman Gilani. The fourth, Navjot Sandhu aka Afsan, wife of Shaukat Hussain Guru, was convicted for a lesser offence. The conviction of Gilani, Afzal and Shaukat was the first such under the Prevention of Terrorism Act (POTA). The trial took place in a speedy manner.

In its order, the Special Court held Mohammed Afzal, Shaukat Hussain Guru and Syed Abdul Rehman Gilani guilty under Sections 121, 121A and 122 of the Indian Penal Code (IPC). They were also found guilty under Section 302, 307, 120B, and Section 3, Subsections 2 and 5 of POTA, besides Section 3, 4 of Explosive Substances Act. With this order the three accused were sentenced for all the offences with which they were charged.

The Special Judge held the three men along with the five deceased terrorists and three others guilty of conspiring to "capture the Parliament House and kill the Prime Minister and Home Minister and to make hostage all the MPs and the VIPs present." Mohammed Haider, Hamza, Raja and Rana, who carried out the attack on Parliament House, were dead. Three others involved, Maulana Masood Azhar, Ghazi Baba alias Abu Jehadi, and Tariq Ahmed were beyond the reach of Indian law.

Special Judge SN Dhingra gave three of the four accused – Mohammed Afzal, Shaukat Hussain Guru and Syed Abdul Rehman Gilani – in the case the death sentence. In his 22-page order on the sentence (the order holding them guilty ran into another 295 pages), Dhingra wrote, "The act of conspiring with foreign terrorists for attacking Parliament is horrendous ... the murder of the security personnel was cold blooded.... I consider this as the rarest of rare cases where they should be given death penalty."

Delhi High Court Judgement

Delhi High Court acquitted SAR Geelani and Afsan Guru in the December 13 Parliament attack case. The two-judge

Bench, comprising Usha Mehra and Pradeep Nandrajog, however, dismissed the appeals of Mohammed Afzal and Shaukat Hussain Guru, against their conviction under the Prevention of Terrorism Act and the death sentences awarded to them on three counts. The judges also upheld an appeal by the State to increase the sentence on the charge of conspiring to wage war against the State from life to death. Citing a Supreme Court judgment of 2002, they held that –

> the offence is of a magnitude that the collective conscious of the community is so shocked that it will expect the holders of the judicial power centre to inflict death penalty irrespective of their personal opinion as regards desirability or otherwise of retaining the death penalty.

Supreme Court Judgement

The Delhi Police appealed to the apex court against the High Court verdict and the Supreme Court has basically upheld the High Court verdict and has also reduced the sentence of Shaukat Hussain Guru.

Nearly four years after the attack on Parliament that shook the nation, the Supreme Court acquitted SAR Gilani, reduced the death sentence to Shaukat Guru to 10 years imprisonment, while upholding the death sentence for Mohammed Afzal. The fourth accused in the case, Shaukat's wife Afsan Guru, was also acquitted.

The Supreme Court said these circumstances clearly established Afzal's association with the terrorists "in almost every act done by them in order to achieve the objective of attacking the Parliament." "Short of participating in the actual attack," Afzal, the Apex Court said, "did everything to set in motion the diabolic mission."

> The gravity of the crime ... is something which cannot be described in words. The incident, which resulted in heavy casualties, had shaken the entire nation and the collective conscience of the society will only be satisfied

if the capital punishment is awarded to the offender. The challenge to the unity, integrity and sovereignty of India ... can only be compensated by giving the maximum punishment.... The appellant, who is a surrendered militant and who was bent upon repeating the acts of treason against the nation, is a menace to the society and his life should become extinct. Accordingly, we uphold the death sentence.

8

Pokhran-II

Pokhran-II was the series of five nuclear bomb test explosions conducted by India at the Indian Army's Pokhran Test Range in May 1998. It was the second Indian nuclear test; the first test, codenamed 'Smiling Buddha', was conducted in May 1974.

Pokhran-II consisted of five detonations, of which the first was a fusion bomb and the remaining four were fission bombs. These nuclear tests resulted in a variety of sanctions against India by a number of major states, including Japan and the United States.

On 11 May 1998, Operation Shakti (Pokhran-II) was initiated with the detonation of one fusion and two fission bombs; the word 'Shakti' means Power. On 13 May 1998, two additional fission devices were detonated, and the government led by Prime Minister Atal Bihari Vajpayee shortly convened a Press Conference to declare that India is a full-fledged nuclear state.

Many names are attributed to these tests; originally they were called Operation Shakti-98 (Power-98), and the five nuclear bombs were designated Shakti-I through Shakti-V. More recently, the operation as a whole has come to be known as Pokhran-II, and the 1974 explosion as Pokhran-I.

Nuclear Bomb Project

Efforts towards building the nuclear bomb, infrastructure, and research on related technologies have been undertaken by India since World War II. Origins of India's nuclear programme dates back to 1944 when nuclear physicist Homi Bhabha began persuading the Indian Congress towards the harnessing of nuclear energy – a year later he established the Tata Institute of Fundamental Research (TIFR).

In 1950s, the preliminary studies were carried out at the BARC and plans were developed to produce plutonium and other bomb components. In 1962, India and China engaged in the disputed northern front, and was further intimidated with Chinese nuclear test in 1964. Direction towards militarisation of the nuclear programme slowed down when Vikram Sarabhai became its head and little interest of Prime Minister Lal Bahadur Shastri in 1965.

After Indira Gandhi became Prime Minister in 1966, the nuclear programme was consolidated when physicist Raja Ramanna joined the efforts. Another nuclear test by China eventually led to India's decision toward building nuclear weapons in 1967 and conducted its first nuclear test, Smiling Buddha, in 1974.

Post-Smiling Buddha

Responding to 'Smiling Buddha', the Nuclear Suppliers Group (NSG) severely affected the India's nuclear programme. The world's major nuclear powers imposed technological embargo on India and Pakistan, which was technologically racing to meet with India's challenge. The nuclear programme struggled for years to gain credibility and its progress crippled by the lack of indigenous resources and dependent on imported technology and technical assistance. At IAEA, Prime Minister Indira Gandhi declared that India's nuclear programme was not militarising despite authorising preliminary work on the hydrogen bomb design.

As an aftermath of the state emergency in 1975 that resulted in the collapse of the Prime Minister Indira Gandhi's government, the nuclear programme was left with a vacuum of political leadership and even basic management. Work on the hydrogen bomb design continued under M Srinivasan, a mechanical engineer, but progress was slow.

The nuclear programme received little attention from Prime Minister Morarji Desai who was renowned for his peace advocacy. In 1978, Prime Minister Desai transferred physicist Ramanna to Indian MoD, and his government was not entirely without progress in nuclear programme and had the programme continue to grow at a desirable rate.

Disturbing news came from Pakistan when the world discovered the Pakistan's clandestine atomic bomb programme. Contrary to India's nuclear programme, Pakistan's atomic bomb programme was akin to United States's Manhattan Project, it was under military oversight with civilian scientists in charge of the scientific aspects of the programme. The Pakistani atomic bomb programme was well funded and organised by then; India realised that Pakistan was likely to succeed in its project in matter of two years.

In 1980, the general elections marked the return of Indira Gandhi and the nuclear programme began to gain momentum under Ramanna in 1981. Requests for additional nuclear tests were continued to be denied by the government when Prime Minister Indira Gandhi saw Pakistan began exercising the brinkmanship, though the nuclear programme continued to advance. Initiation towards hydrogen bomb began as well as the launch of the missile programme began under late President Dr Abdul Kalam, who was then an aerospace engineer.

Political Momentum 1988-1998

In 1989, the general elections witnessed the Janata Dal party led by VP Singh, forming the government. Prime

Minister VP Singh down played the relations with the Prime Minister Benazir Bhutto whose Pakistan Peoples Party (PPP) won the general elections in 1988. Foreign relations between India and Pakistan began to severely worsen when India began charging Pakistan of supporting the militancy in Jammu and Kashmir. During this time, the missile programme succeeded in the development of the Prithvi missiles.

Successive governments in India decided to observe this temporary moratorium for fear of inviting international criticism. The Indian public had been supportive towards the nuclear tests which ultimately led Prime Minister Narasimha Rao deciding to conduct further tests in 1995. Plans were halted after American spy satellites picked up signs of preparations for nuclear testing at Pokhran Test Range in Rajasthan. President Bill Clinton and his administration exerted enormous pressure on Prime Minister Narasimha Rao to stop the preparations. Responding to India, Prime Minister Benazir Bhutto issued harsh and severe statements against India on Pakistan's news channels; thus putting stress on the relations between two countries.

Diplomatic tension escalated between two countries when Prime Minister Benazir Bhutto raised the Kashmir issue at the United Nations in 1995. In a speech delivered by the then Speaker National Assembly Yousaf Raza Gillani, stressed the 'Kashmir issue' as continue to endanger the peace and security in the region. The Indian delegation headed by Atal Bihari Vajpayee at the United Nations, reiterated that the UN resolutions only call upon Pakistan - the occupying force to vacate the "Jammu and Kashmir Area".

General Elections 1998

The BJP, came to power in 1998 general elections with an exclusive public mandate. BJP's political might had been growing steadily in strength over the past decade over several issues.

In Pakistan, the similar conservative force, the PML(N), was also in power with an exclusive mandate led by Prime Minister Nawaz Sharif who defeated the leftist PPP led by Benazir Bhutto in general elections held in 1997. During the BJP campaign, Atal Bihari Vajpayee indulged in grand standing – such as when he declared on 25 February that his government would "take back that part of Kashmir that is under Pakistan's control." Before this declaration, the BJP platform had clear intention to "exercise the option to induct nuclear weapons" and "India should become an openly nuclear power to garner the respect on the world stage that India deserved." By 18 March 1998, Vajpayee had publicly begun his lobbying for nuclear explosion and declared that "there is no compromise on national security; all options including the nuclear options will be exercised to protect security and sovereignty."

Consultation began between Prime Minister Vajpayee, Dr Abdul Kalam, R Chidambaram and officials of the Indian DAE on nuclear options. Chidambaram briefed Prime Minister Vajpayee extensively on the nuclear programme; Abdul Kalam presented the status of the missile programme. On 28 March 1998, Prime Minister Vajpayee asked the scientists to make preparations in the shortest time possible, and preparations were hastily made.

It was time of tense atmosphere when Pakistan, at a Conference on Disarmament, offered a peace rhetoric agreement with India for "an equal and mutual restraint in conventional, missile and nuclear fields." Pakistan's equation was later re-emphasised on 6 April and the momentum in India for nuclear tests began to build up which strengthened Vajpayee's position to order the tests.

Preparations for the Test

Unlike Pakistan's weapon-testing laboratories, there was very little that India could do to hide its activity at Pokhran. Contrary to high-altitude granite mountains in Pakistan, the bushes are sparse and the dunes in the Rajasthan Desert don't provide much cover from probing satellites. The Indian intelligence had been aware of United States spy satellites and the American CIA had been detecting Indian test preparations since 1995; therefore, the tests required complete secrecy in India and also needed to avoid detection by other countries. The 58th Engineer Regiment of Indian Army's Corps of Engineers was commissioned to prepare the test sites without being probed by the United States spy satellites. The 58th Engineer's Commander Colonel Gopal Kaushik supervised the test preparations and ordered his "staff officers take all measures to ensure total secrecy."

Extensive planning was done by a very small group of scientists, senior military officers and senior politicians to ensure that the test preparations would remain secret, and even senior members of the Indian government didn't know what was going on. The Chief Scientific Adviser and the Director of Defence Research and Development Organisation (DRDO), Dr Abdul Kalam, and Dr R Chidambaram, the Director of the Department of Atomic Energy (DAE), were the chief coordinators of this test planning. The scientists and engineers of the Bhabha Atomic Research Centre (BARC), the Atomic Minerals Directorate for Exploration and Research (AMDER), and the Defence Research and Development Organisation (DRDO) were involved in the nuclear weapon assembly, layout, detonation and obtaining test data. A very small group of senior scientists were involved in the detonation process, all scientists were required to wear army uniforms to preserve the secrecy of the tests. Since 1995, the 58th Engineer Regiment had learned to avoid satellite detection. Work was mostly done during night, and equipment was returned to the original place to give the impression that it was never moved.

Bomb shafts were dug under camouflage netting and the dug-out sand was shaped like dunes. Cables for sensors were covered with sand and concealed using native vegetation. Scientists would not depart for Pokhran in groups of two or three. They travelled to destinations other than Pokhran under pseudonyms, and were then transported by the army. Technical staff at the test range wore military uniform, to prevent detection in satellite images.

Development and Test Teams

The main technical personnel involved in the operation were:

- Project Chief Coordinators.
- Dr R Chidambaram, Chairman of the Atomic Energy Commission and the Department of Atomic energy.
- Dr APJ Abdul Kalam (later, President of India), Scientific Adviser to the prime minister and Head of the DRDO.
- Defence Research & Development Organization (DRDO).
- Dr K Santhanam, Director, Test Site Preparations.
- Atomic Minerals Directorate for Exploration and Research.
- Dr GR Dikshitulu; Senior Research Scientist BSOI Group, Nuclear Materials Acquisition.
- Bhabha Atomic Research Centre (BARC).
- Dr Anil Kakodkar, Director of BARC.
- Dr Satinder Kumar Sikka, Director; Thermonuclear Weapon Development.
- Dr MS Ramakumar, Director of Nuclear Fuel and Automation Manufacturing Group; Director, Nuclear Component Manufacture.
- Dr DD Sood, Director of Radiochemistry and Isotope Group; Director, Nuclear Materials Acquisition.
- Dr SK Gupta, Solid State Physics and Spectroscopy Group; Director, Device Design & Assessment.

- Dr G Govindraj, Associate Director of Electronic and Instrumentation Group; Director, Field Instrumentation.

Movement and Logistics

Three laboratories of the DRDO were involved in designing, testing and producing components for the bombs, including the advanced detonators, the implosion and high-voltage trigger systems. These were also responsible for weaponising, systems engineering, aerodynamics, safety interlocks and flight trials. The bombs were transported in four Indian Army trucks under the command of Colonel Umang Kapur; all devices from BARC were relocated at 3 am on 1 May 1998. From the Chhatrapati Shivaji International Airport, the bombs were flown in an Indian Air Force's AN-32 plane to the Jaisalmer army base. They were transported to Pokhran in an army convoy of four trucks, and this required three trips. The devices were delivered to the device preparation building, which was designated as 'Prayer Hall'.

The test sites was organised into two government groups and were fired separately, with all devices in a group fired at the same time. The first group consisted of the thermonuclear device (Shakti I), the fission device (Shakti II), and a sub-kiloton device (Shakti III). The second group consisted of the remaining two sub-kiloton devices Shakti IV and V. It was decided that the first group would be tested on 11 May and the second group on 13 May. The thermonuclear device was placed in a shaft code named 'White House', which was over 200 metres (660 ft) deep, the fission bomb was placed in a 150 metres (490 ft) deep shaft code named 'Taj Mahal', and the first sub-kiloton device in 'Kumbhkaran'. The first three devices were placed in their respective shafts on 10 May, and the first device to be placed was the sub-kiloton device in the 'Kumbhkaran' shaft, which was sealed by the army engineers by 8:30 PM. The thermonuclear device was lowered and sealed into the 'White House' shaft by 4 AM, and the fission device being placed in the 'Taj Mahal' shaft was sealed at 7:30 AM, which was 90 minutes before the planned test time. The shafts were L-shaped, with a horizontal chamber for the test device.

The timing of the tests depended on the local weather conditions, with the wind being the critical factor. The tests were underground, but due to a number of shaft seal failures that had occurred during tests conducted by the United States, the Soviet Union, and the United Kingdom, the sealing of the shaft could not be guaranteed to be leak-proof. By early afternoon, the winds had died down and the test sequence was initiated. Dr K Santhanam of the DRDO, in charge of the test site preparations, gave the two keys that activated the test countdown to Dr M Vasudev, the Range Safety Officer, who was responsible for verifying that all test indicators were normal. After checking the indicators, Vasudev handed one key each to a representative of BARC and the DRDO, who unlocked the countdown system together. At 3:45 PM the three devices were detonated.

Nuclear Bombs and Detonations

Five nuclear devices were made during Operation Shakti. All devices were weapon-grade plutonium and they were:

- Shakti I – A thermonuclear device yielding 45 kt, but designed for up to 200 kt.
- Shakti II – A plutonium implosion design yielding 15 kt and intended as a warhead that could be delivered by bomber or missile. It was an improvement of the device detonated in the 1974 Smiling Buddha (Pokhran-I) test of 1974, developed using simulations on the PARAM supercomputer.
- Shakti III – An experimental linear implosion design that used "non-weapon grade" plutonium, but which likely omitted the material required for fusion, yielding 0.3 kt.

- Shakti IV - A 0.5 kt experimental device.
- Shakti V - A 0.2 kt experimental device.

An additional, sixth device (Shakti VI) is suspected to have been present but not detonated.

At 3:43 PM IST; three nuclear bombs (specifically, the Shakti I, II and III) were detonated simultaneously, as measured by international seismic monitors. On 13 May, at 12.21 PM IST 6:51 UTC, two sub-kiloton devices (Shakti IV and V) were detonated. Due to their very low yield, these explosions were not detected by any seismic station. On 13 May 1998, India declared the series of tests to be over after this.

Following the Pokhran-II tests, India became the sixth country to join the nuclear club. Shortly after the tests, a press meet was convened at the Prime Minister's residence in New Delhi. Prime Minister Atal Bihari Vajpayee appeared before the press corps and made the following short statement:

> Today, at 15:45 hours, India conducted three underground nuclear tests in the Pokhran range. The tests conducted today were with a fission device, a low yield device and a thermonuclear device. The measured yields are in line with expected values. Measurements have also confirmed that there was no release of radioactivity into the atmosphere. These were contained explosions like the experiment conducted in May 1974. I warmly congratulate the scientists and engineers who have carried out these successful tests.

News of the tests were greeted with jubilation and large-scale approval by society in India. The Bombay Stock Exchange registered significant gains. Newspapers and television channels praised the government for its bold decision; editorials were full of praise for the country's leadership and advocated the development of an operational nuclear arsenal for the country's armed forces. The Indian opposition, led by Congress party criticised the Vajpayee administration for carrying out the series of nuclear tests. The Congress Party spokesman, Salman Khursheed, accused the BJP of trying to use the tests for political ends rather than to enhance the country's national security.

By the time India had conducted tests, the country had a total of $ 44 billion in loans in 1998, from IMF and the World Bank. The industrial sectors of the Indian economy such as the chemicals industry, were likely to be hurt by sanctions. The Western consortium companies, which had invested heavily in India, especially in construction, computing and telecoms, were generally the ones who were harmed by the sanctions. In 1998, Indian government announced that it had already allowed for some economic response and was willing to take the consequences.

International Reactions

United States

The United States issued a strong statement condemning India and promised that sanctions would follow. The American intelligence community was embarrassed as there had been "a serious intelligence failure of the decade" in detecting the preparations for the test.

In keeping with its preferred approach to foreign policy in recent decades, and in compliance with the 1994 anti-proliferation law, the United States imposed economic sanctions on India. The sanctions on India consisted of cutting off all assistance to India except humanitarian aid, banning the export of certain defence material and technologies, ending American credit and credit guarantees to India, and requiring the US to oppose lending by international financial institutions to India.

From 1998-1999, the United States held series of bilateral talks with India over the issue of India becoming party of the CTBT and NPT. In addition, the United States also made an unsuccessful attempt of holding talks regarding the rollback of India's nuclear programme. India took a firm stand against the CTBT and refusing to be signatory party of it despite under pressure by the US President Bill Clinton, and noted the treaty as it was not consistent with India's national security interest.

Canada, Japan and Other Countries

Strong criticism was drawn from Canada on India's actions and its High Commissioner. Sanctions were also imposed by Japan on India and consisted of freezing all new loans and grants except for humanitarian aid to India.

Some other nations also imposed sanctions on India, primarily in the form of suspension of foreign aid to India and government-to-government credit lines. However, the United Kingdom, France, and Russia refrained from condemning India.

UN Sanctions

The reactions from abroad started immediately after the tests were advertised. On 6 June, the United Nations Security Council adopted Resolution 1172 condemning the test and that of Pakistan's. China issued a vociferous condemnation calling upon the international community to exert pressure on India to sign the NPT and eliminate its nuclear arsenal. With India joining the group of countries possessing nuclear weapons, a new strategic dimension had emerged in Asia, particularly South Asia.

Effects on Indian Economy

Overall, the effect of international sanctions on Indian economy was minimal; the technological progress was marginal. Most nations did not call for embargoes against India as the exports and imports together constituted only 4.0% of its GDP, with United States trade accounting for only 10.0% of this total. Far more significant were the restrictions on lending imposed by the United States and its representatives on international finance bodies. Most of the sanctions were lifted within five years.

The Indian government has officially declared the 11th May as National Technology Day in India to commemorate the first of the five nuclear tests that were carried out on 11 May 1998.

It was officially signed by the then Prime Minister Atal Bihari Vajpayee in 1998 and the day is celebrated by giving awards to various individuals and industries in the field of science and technology.

9

अटलजी की कविताएँ

मौत से ठन गई!

ठन गई!

मौत से ठन गई!

जूझने का मेरा इरादा न था,
मोड़ पर मिलेंगे इसका वादा न था,

रास्ता रोक कर वह खड़ी हो गई,
यों लगा ज़िन्दगी से बड़ी हो गई।

मौत की उमर क्या है? दो पल भी नहीं,
ज़िन्दगी सिलसिला, आज कल की नहीं।

मैं जी भर जिया, मैं मन से मरूँ,
लौटकर आऊँगा, कूच से क्यों डरूँ?

तू दबे पाँव, चोरी-छिपे से न आ,
सामने वार कर फिर मुझे आज़मा।

मौत से बेख़बर, जिन्दगी का सफ़र,
शाम हर सुरमई, रात बंसी का स्वर।

बात ऐसी नहीं कि कोई ग़म ही नहीं,
दर्द अपने-पराए कुछ कम भी नहीं।

प्यार इतना परायों से मुझको मिला,
न अपनों से बाक़ी है कोई गिला।

हर चुनौती से दो हाथ मैंने किये,
आंधियों में जलाए हैं बुझते दिए।

आज झकझोरता तेज़ तूफ़ान है,
नाव भँवरों की बाँहों में मेहमान है।

पार पाने का क़ायम मगर हौसला,
देख तेवर तूफ़ाँ का, तेवरी तन गई।

मौत से ठन गई।

हार नहीं मानूँगा

राहों में फैली सिर्फ मुश्किलें।
बंद हैं सारे दरवाज़े।
किसी तरह दरवाज़ा खोलूँगा।
हार नहीं मानूँगा।

परेशान है मन।
थक चुका है पूरा तन।
अंधकारमय हो गया है जीवन।
इस अंधकार में प्रकाश तलाशूँगा।
हार नहीं मानूँगा।
मैं हार नहीं मानूँगा।

साथ छूटे तो क्या हुआ।
रिश्ते टूटे तो क्या हुआ।
अकेले रहकर ही मैं अकेलेपन को मारूँगा।

लेकिन ...
हार नहीं मानूँगा।
मैं हार नहीं मानूँगा।
मुश्किल है मंज़िल तो क्या।
मुसीबत का अम्बार लगे तो क्या।
राह में पत्थर फैले तो क्या।
उसी पत्थर से मैं सड़क बनाऊँगा।
अपनी मंज़िल पा कर रहूँगा।
पर मैं ...
हार नहीं मानूँगा।
मैं हार नहीं मानूँगा।
धुन्ध का समन्दर है।
ना राह है ना राहगीर।
वीरान सा जहाँ है।
इसी वीराने में आशियाना बनाऊँगा।
पर ...
मैं हार नहीं मानूँगा।
मैं हार नहीं मानूँगा।
तप रहा है सारा संसार।
भंवर में खोया है हर एक परिवार।
इंसान तो हैं पर इंसानियत नहीं।
भीड़ तो है पर अपनापन नहीं।
दुनिया जल रही है हर वक्त।
बदल रही है ज़िन्दगी करवट हर वक्त।
जलना पड़े तो जलूँगा।
मुश्किलों को मारने के लिए खुद को जलाऊँगा।
आग की भट्टी में स्वयं तपाऊँगा।
पर मैं ...
हार नहीं मानूँगा।
मैं हार नहीं मानूँगा।

गीत नया गाता हूँ

टूटे हुए तारों से फूटे बासंती स्वर
पत्थर की छाती मे उग आया नव अंकुर
झरे सब पीले पात कोयल की कुहुक रात
प्राची मे अरुणिम की रेख देख पता हूँ
गीत नया गाता हूँ
टूटे हुए सपनों की कौन सुने सिसकी
अन्तर की चीर व्यथा पलको पर ठिठकी
हार नहीं मानूँगा, रार नहीं ठानूँगा,
काल के कपाल पे लिखता मिटाता हूँ
गीत नया गाता हूँ

क़दम मिला कर चलना होगा

बाधाएँ आती हैं आएँ
घिरें प्रलय की घोर घटाएँ,
पावों के नीचे अंगारे,
सिर पर बरसें यदि ज्वालाएँ,
निज हाथों में हँसते-हँसते,
आग लगाकर जलना होगा।
क़दम मिलाकर चलना होगा।

हास्य-रुदन में, तूफ़ानों में,
अगर असंख्यक बलिदानों में,
उद्यानों में, वीरानों में,
अपमानों में, सम्मानों में,
उन्नत मस्तक, उभरा सीना,
पीड़ाओं में पलना होगा।
क़दम मिलाकर चलना होगा।

उजियारे में, अंधकार में,
कल कहार में, बीच धार में,
घोर घृणा में, पूत प्यार में,
क्षणिक जीत में, दीर्घ हार में,
जीवन के शत-शत आकर्षक,
अरमानों को ढलना होगा।
क़दम मिलाकर चलना होगा।

सम्मुख फैला अगर ध्येय पथ,
प्रगति चिरंतन कैसा इति अब,
सुस्मित हर्षित कैसा श्रम श्लथ,
असफल, सफल समान मनोरथ,
सब कुछ देकर कुछ न मांगते,
पावस बनकर ढ़लना होगा।
क़दम मिलाकर चलना होगा।

कुछ काँटों से सज्जित जीवन,
प्रखर प्यार से वंचित यौवन,
नीरवता से मुखरित मधुबन,
परहित अर्पित अपना तन-मन,
जीवन को शत-शत आहुति में,
जलना होगा, गलना होगा।
क़दम मिलाकर चलना होगा।

दो अनुभूतियां

(१)

बेनकाब चेहरे हैं, दाग बड़े गहरे हैं
टूटता तिलिस्म आज सच से भय खाता हूं
गीत नहीं गाता हूं

लगी कुछ ऐसी नज़र बिखरा शीशे सा शहर
अपनों के मेले में मीत नहीं पाता हूं
गीत नहीं गाता हूं

पीठ मे छुरी सा चांद, राहू गया रेखा फांद
मुक्ति के क्षणों में बार बार बंध जाता हूं
गीत नहीं गाता हूं

(२)

गीत नया गाता हूं

टूटे हुए तारों से फूटे बासंती स्वर
पत्थर की छाती मे उग आया नव अंकुर
झरे सब पीले पात कोयल की कुहुक रात

प्राची मे अरुणिम की रेख देख पता हूं
गीत नया गाता हूं

टूटे हुए सपनों की कौन सुने सिसकी
अन्तर की चीर व्यथा पलकों पर ठिठकी
हार नहीं मानूंगा, रार नहीं ठानूंगा,

काल के कपाल पे लिखता मिटाता हूं
गीत नया गाता हूं

मनाली मत जइयो

मनाली मत जइयो, गोरी
राजा के राज में।

जइयो तो जइयो,
उड़िके मत जइयो,

अधर में लटकीहौ,
वायुदूत के जहाज़ में।

जइयो तो जइयो,
सन्देसा न पइयो,
टेलिफोन बिगड़े हैं,
मिर्धा महाराज में।

जइयो तो जइयो,
मशाल ले के जइयो,
बिजुरी भइ बैरिन
अंधेरिया रात में।

जइयो तो जइयो,
त्रिशूल बांध जइयो,
मिलेंगे ख़ालिस्तानी,
राजीव के राज में।

मनाली तो जइहो।
सुरग सुख पइहों।
दुख नीको लागे, मोहे
राजा के राज में।

दूध में दरार पड़ गई

खून क्यों सफेद हो गया?

भेद में अभेद खो गया।
बंट गये शहीद, गीत कट गए,
कलेजे में कटार दड़ गई।
दूध में दरार पड़ गई।

खेतों में बारूदी गंध,
टूट गये नानक के छंद
सतलुज सहम उठी, व्यथित सी बितस्ता है।
वसंत से बहार झड़ गई
दूध में दरार पड़ गई।

अपनी ही छाया से बैर,
गले लगने लगे हैं ग़ैर,
ख़ुदकुशी का रास्ता, तुम्हें वतन का वास्ता।
बात बनाएं, बिगड़ गई।
दूध में दरार पड़ गई।

एक बरस बीत गया

झुलासाता जेठ मास
शरद चांदनी उदास
सिसकी भरते सावन का
अंतर्घट रीत गया
एक बरस बीत गया

सीकचों मे सिमटा जग
किंतु विकल प्राण विहग
धरती से अम्बर तक
गूंज मुक्ति गीत गया
एक बरस बीत गया

पथ निहारते नयन
गिनते दिन पल छिन
लौट कभी आएगा
मन का जो मीत गया
एक बरस बीत गया

ऊँचाई

ऊँचे पहाड़ पर,
पेड़ नहीं लगते,
पौधे नहीं उगते,
न घास ही जमती है।

जमती है सिर्फ बर्फ,
जो, कफन की तरह सफेद और,
मौत की तरह ठंडी होती है।
खेलती, खिल-खिलाती नदी,
जिसका रूप धारण कर,
अपने भाग्य पर बूंद-बूंद रोती है।

ऐसी ऊँचाई,
जिसका परस
पानी को पत्थर कर दे,
ऐसी ऊँचाई
जिसका दरस हीन भाव भर दे,
अभिनन्दन की अधिकारी है,
आरोहियों के लिये आमंत्रण है,
उस पर झंडे गाड़े जा सकते हैं,

किन्तु कोई गौरैया,
वहाँ नीड़ नहीं बना सकती,
ना कोई थका-मांदा बटोही,
उसकी छांव में पलभर पलक ही झपका सकता है।

सच्चाई यह है कि
केवल ऊँचाई ही काफी नहीं होती,
सबसे अलग-थलग,
परिवेश से पृथक,
अपनों से कटा-बंटा,

शून्य में अकेला खड़ा होना,
पहाड़ की महानता नहीं,
मजबूरी है।
ऊँचाई और गहराई में
आकाश-पाताल की दूरी है।

जो जितना ऊँचा,
उतना एकाकी होता है,
हर भार को स्वयं ढोता है,
चेहरे पर मुस्कानें चिपका,
मन ही मन रोता है।

जरूरी यह है कि
ऊँचाई के साथ विस्तार भी हो,
जिससे मनुष्य,
ठूंट सा खड़ा न रहे,
औरों से घुले-मिले,
किसी को साथ ले,
किसी के संग चले।

भीड़ में खो जाना,
यादों में डूब जाना,
स्वयं को भूल जाना,
अस्तित्व को अर्थ,
जीवन को सुगंध देता है।

धरती को बौनों की नहीं,
ऊँचे कद के इन्सानों की जरूरत है।
इतने ऊँचे कि आसमान छू लें,
नये नक्षत्रों में प्रतिभा की बीज बो लें,

किन्तु इतने ऊँचे भी नहीं,
कि पाँव तले दूब ही न जमे,

कोई कांटा न चुभे,
कोई कलि न खिले।

न वसंत हो, न पतझड़,
हो सिर्फ ऊँचाई का अंधड़,
मात्र अकेलेपन का सन्नाटा।

मेरे प्रभु!
मुझे इतनी ऊँचाई कभी मत देना,
गैरों को गले न लगा सकूँ,
इतनी रुखाई कभी मत देना।

हरी-हरी दूब पर

हरी-हरी दूब पर
ओस की बूंदे
अभी थी,
अभी नहीं हैं।
ऐसी खुशियाँ
जो हमेशा हमारा साथ दें
कभी नहीं थी,
कहीं नहीं हैं।

क्काँयर की कोख से
फूटा बाल सूर्य,
जब पूरब की गोद में
पाँव फैलाने लगा,
तो मेरी बगीची का
पत्ता-पत्ता जगमगाने लगा,
मैं उगते सूर्य को नमस्कार.करूँ
या उसके ताप से भाप बनी,
ओस की बूँदों को ढूंढूँ?

सूर्य एक सत्य है
जिसे झुठलाया नहीं जा सकता
मगर ओस भी तो एक सच्चाई है
यह बात अलग है कि ओस क्षणिक है
क्यों न मैं क्षण क्षण को जिऊँ?
कण-कण में बिखरे सौन्दर्य को पिऊँ?

सूर्य तो फिर भी उगेगा,
धूप तो फिर भी खिलेगी,
लेकिन मेरी बगीची की
हरी-हरी दूब पर,
ओस की बूँद
हर मौसम में नहीं मिलेगी।

क्षमा याचना

क्षमा करो बापू! तुम हमको,
बचन भंग के हम अपराधी,
राजघाट को किया अपावन,
मंज़िल भूले, यात्रा आधी।

जयप्रकाश जी! रखो भरोसा,
टूटे सपनों को जोड़ेंगे।
चिताभस्म की चिंगारी से,
अन्धकार के गढ़ तोड़ेंगे।

Homage

Atalji's death is of course a personal loss for you and others at home. It is also a personal loss for me. It was his stature and dignity that attracted me to public life, as I gave up the legal profession to become his colleague.

Years later, when I called on him after being elected the President of India, he was bed-ridden but responded as only he could with a movement of his eyes. Silently I felt he blessed me.

He was our much-loved former Prime Minister, a national leader of rare distinction and a statesman of modern India. In his long and distinguished public career, he touched innumerable lives in innumerable ways – as a freedom fighter and an intellectual, as a writer and a poet, as a parliamentarian and an administrator and finally as Prime Minister. He was truly the Renaissance Man of Indian politics.

Extremely sad to hear of the passing of Shri Atal Bihari Vajpayee, our former Prime Minister and a true Indian statesman. His leadership, foresight, maturity and eloquence put him in a league of his own. Atalji, the Gentle Giant, will be missed by one and all.

Ràm Nath Kovind, President

Deeply saddened at the passing away of Shri Atal Bihari Vajpayee. A reasoned critique in opposition and a seeker of consensus as PM, Atalji was a democrat to the core. In his passing away, India has lost a great son and an era has come to an end. My deepest condolences.

Though he was suffering for a long time I did not believe that the end will come. Fate snatched him away from us. He carried conviction with everybody. No doubt that the country will be poorer in the loss of Atal Bihari Vajpayee who was like a colossus for almost 6 decades. I pay my deepest regards for this great son of India.

Pranab Mukherjee, Former President

Sad to know that Shri Atalji is no more. I visited him today morning but didn't imagine that the end will come so soon. He is, undoubtedly, one of the tallest leaders in post-Independence India.

His contribution to strengthen democracy and good governance has been stupendous. He successfully ran a coalition of 23 parties with his rare persuasive charm and competence.

He will be remembered for ushering in the connectivity revolution in the country. 'Bharat Ratna' Shri Atal Bihari Vajpayee's qualities of Vyakthitva (personality), Vakthruthva (oratory), Karthruthva (devotion to duty), Mithrutva (friendliness) all combined in his remarkable 'Nethrutva' will be remembered for a long time to come.

He was a true Indian. He never hesitated to speak from his heart. Vajpayeeji is 'Ajatshatru' of modern times because he always maintained dignity and decorum.

Venkaiah Naidu, Vice-President

Atal Bihari Vajpayee was an eminent statesman known for his wisdom moderation intact. His way of communication was unique and made him extremely popular. This kind of a person comes once in a blue moon. He will be remembered for a long time.

Mohd Hamid Ansari, Former Vice-President

Atalji was like a star in the sky of politics, which shone brighter than everyone else. He had the unique ability to bring everyone together. Even if you ask the opposition they hold a sense of respect for him.

Sumitra Mahajan, Speaker, Lok Sabha

His death is a void that will never be filled. I have lost a father figure today. Atalji taught me valuable aspects about Sangathan and Shaasan.

We have lost our inspiration. We have lost an Atal Ratna. The personality of Atalji and the sadness due to his demise can't be described in words.

He was a wonderful orator, a prolific writer and he dutifully served our country.

It was due to the perseverance and struggles of Atalji that the BJP was built brick by brick. He travelled across the length and breadth of India to spread the BJP's message, which led to the BJP becoming a strong force in our national polity and in several states.

Atalji's passing away is a personal and irreplaceable loss for me. I have countless fond memories with him. He was an inspiration to Karyakartas like me. I will particularly remember his sharp intellect and outstanding wit.

It was Atalji's exemplary leadership that set the foundations for a strong, prosperous and inclusive India in the 21st century. His futuristic policies across various sectors touched the lives of each and every citizen of India.

India grieves the demise of our beloved Atalji. His passing away marks the end of an era. He lived for the nation and served it assiduously for decades. My thoughts are with his family, BJP Karyakartas and millions of admirers in this hour of sadness. Om Shanti.

Atalji, you will live on in the hearts and minds of every Indian. No words can ever do justice to your rich contribution towards the making of our country.

Narendra Modi, Prime Minister

He was a true parliamentarian. With his death, a vacuum has been created in polity and end of an era of politics in this country. He was a great orator who refused to attack hisopponent personally.

Deve Gowda, Former Prime Minister

Vajpayeeji was a great patriot and was one of the greatest leaders of India. He stood among the tallest leaders of modern India who spent his whole life serving our country.

He was an excellent orator, an impressive poet, an exceptional public servant, an outstanding Parliamentarian and a great Prime Minister of India. Vajpayeeji was a great statesman and he proved his ability both on national and international level, by improving our relationship with all the countries, especially with our neighbouring countries.

His ability and personality were such that people from all walks of life, irrespective of their political leanings, loved and respected Vajpayeeji. His services to our nation will be remembered for a long time to come.

Manmohan Singh, Former Prime Minister

Atal Behari Vajpayee was one of the most towering political geniuses to have dominated the political space in India after Independence. He was a consummate Parliamentarian, an astute statesman, an orator par excellence and a warm-hearted person.

C Vidyasagar Rao, Governor, Maharashtra

Saddened over the demise of a visionary leader Sh. Atal Bihari Vajpayeeji, former Prime Minister of India. Pray for peace to the departed soul and strength to the bereaved family members.

NN Vohra, Former Governor, J&K

My ever inspiring leader, statesman par excellence, mentor has left the mortal world. Atalji apostle Ajathshatru will forever shine on planet earth as harbinger of peace and harmony.

My tributes to the great versatile personality whom we all always called as "Babjee".

END OF AN ERA - India will be poorer with the passing away of a legend - who strode the political domain like a polestar icon and guiding star forever.

Ananth Kumar, Minister of Chemicals and Fertilizers and Parliamentary Affairs

Saddened by the demise of Atalji, unquestionably one of the tallest leaders of India. His contribution to India and India's democracy will be always remembered.

His vision, oration, poetry, blended with his national commitment earned him respect from both friends and opponents.

Arun Jaitley, Finance Minister

युगपुरुष एवं भारत रत्न से सम्मानित आदरणीय श्री अटल बिहारी वाजपेयीजी के निधन से भारत को अपूर्णीय क्षति हुई है जिसे शब्दों में बयान नहीं किया जा सकता। दिवंगत आत्मा की शांति की प्रार्थना करता हूं।

Birender Singh, Minister of Steel

An extraordinary leader of India's freedom movement who, among his great achievements, thrusted India into the nuclear club, Shri Atal Bihari Vajpayee ji will be remembered forever as man of great talents yet a simple and humble demeanour.

Dharmendra Pradhan, Minister of Petroleum & Natural Gas and Skill Development & Entrepreneurship

A visionary statesman, with political sagacity, his acceptability across diverse ideological spectrum endeared him to all.

Harsh Vardhan, Minister of - Science & Technology; Environment, Forest & Climate Change; and Earth Sciences

We grew up listening to him, learning from him, inspired by him. There was no electronic media those days, but many of our college-mates, who did not subscribe to our ideology, would come over to his rallies, just to pick up speaking skills from his oratory.

Jitendra Singh, Minister of State (Independent Charge) for the Ministry of Development of North-Eastern Region ...

Lost words on the demise of Atal Bihari Vajpayeeji. "A great man is one who leaves others at a loss after he is gone" and "The greatness of a man is measured by the way he treats the little man."

His last 2006 interview for an ordinary person like me!

Tribute to the great soul.

Kiren Rijiju, Minister of State for Home

परम श्रद्धेय श्री अटल बिहारी वाजपेयीजी के जाने से भारतीय राजनीति का एक ऐसा स्थान रिक्त हो गया है, जिसे भरा नहीं जा सकता। ईश्वर वाजपेयीजी की आत्मा को शांति प्रदान करें और समस्त भारतीय जनता पार्टी परिवार को यह दुख सहन करने का धैर्य, साहस और संबल प्रदान करें।

Maneka Gandhi, Minister for Women and Child Development

Atalji "Atal The, Atal Hain aur Atal Rahenge". Jab Tak Sooraj-Chand Rahega, Atalji Ka Naam Rahega, Kaam Rahega. My tributes.

Mukhtar Abbas Naqvi, Minister for Minority Affairs

श्रद्धेय अटलजी का देहावसान हम सभी के लिए अपूर्णनीय क्षति है। अटलजी छात्र जीवन से ही मेरे लिए आदर्श रहे हैं। प्रधानमंत्री स्वर्णिम चतुर्भुज सड़क योजना और प्रधानमंत्री ग्रामीण सड़क योजना के क्रियान्वयन में उनके साथ काम करने का मौका मिला। मैं भाजपा अध्यक्ष बना, उस समय भी अटलजी से मुझे भावनात्मक जिम्मेदारी का अहसास मिला। हम सरकार भी उनके दिखाये रास्ते पर चलाने की कोशिश कर रहे हैं। भाजपा का संसद में 2 सदस्यों से बहुमत तक पहुँचाना अटलजी के प्रेरणादायी नेतृत्व और आशीष से ही सम्भव हो सका। वह महानायक और अजातशत्रु हैं। वह हम सब में आत्मबल के रूप में सिर्फ और सिर्फ अटल हैं। अटल जी अजर-अमर हैं। उन्हें मेरी भावभीनी श्रद्धांजलि है। ॐ

Nitin Gadkari, Union Minister of Road Transport and Highways and Shipping

अटलजी ने पूरा जीवन राष्ट्र की सेवा की और हम सभी का मार्गदर्शन किया। भगवान रंजन, नमिता और निहारिका को दुःख की इस कठिन घड़ी से उबरने की शक्ति प्रदान करें।

श्रद्धेय अटल बिहारी वाजपेयीजी का जाना एक युग का अंत है। अटलजी का महान व्यक्तित्व, सौम्य शैली, राष्ट्रभक्ति, दूरदृष्टि, चुनौतियों से सामना करने की दृढ़ इच्छाशक्ति व उनके महान आदर्श हमें सदैव प्रेरणा देंगे। व्यक्तिगत रूप से मेरे लिए यह एक अपूरणीय क्षति है। भावपूर्ण श्रद्धांजलि।

Piyush Goyal, Minister of Railways, Coal and Corporate Affairs

Pained beyond words at the demise of Shri Atalji. He had cherished the ideal of a developed and powerful India in which all persons lived together in unity, peace and harmony.

Atalji was a true 'Ajatshatru' who had many friends across the political spectrum. He believed in political consensus and his beliefs had consequential effect on Indian politics.

Rajnath Singh, Union Home Minister

अपने वचन के पक्के, वादों और इरादों में "अटल" हमारे अटलजी हमारे बीच नहीं रहे।

चाहे पोखरण हो या कारगिल, राष्ट्रनिर्माण में अटल जी का योगदान कृतज्ञता और सम्मान से याद किया जाएगा।

नेता और जनता, सभी के मन में बसते थे हमारे अटल जी। उनका निधन देश के लिए एक बहुत बड़ी क्षति है।

Rajyavardhan Singh Rathore, Minister of State (Independent Charge) for the Ministry of Youth Affairs and Sports

He was a great politician, intense speaker, a true diplomat, having clarity in thinking, warrior of social justice and a great nationalist.

Ram Vilas Paswan, Minister of Consumer Affairs, Food and Public Distribution

Atal ji struggled all his life to uphold the ideals so dear to him, it culminated in his becoming PM in 1996, period of 1998-2004 when he held the position again, will be always remembered Good Governance. Fought with ailments, last few years, today fight ends. We always will miss you.

Suresh Prabhu, Minister of Commerce & Industry and Civil Aviation

With the sad demise of Shri Atal Bihari Vajpayee, an era has ended. He was liked by his opponents and loved by the party cadres. His amiability and generosity were the unique aspects of his personality. My heartfelt tribute to Shri Atalji.

Sushma Swaraj, Minister of External Affairs

Deeply saddened by the demise of our beloved leader & former PM Shri Atal Bihari Vajpayeeji. India has lost one of her most beloved sons, a statesman, and unarguably one of the best PMs to have led the country. Rest In Peace Atalji, we will miss you.

VK Singh, Minister of State for External Affairs

The country has lost a great leader ... and BJP has lost its first national president.

Amit Shah, President, BJP

I am at a loss of words to express my deep grief and sadness today as we all mourn the passing away of one of India's tallest statesmen, Shri Atal Bihari Vajpayee. To me, Atalji was more than a senior colleague - in fact, he was my closest friend for over 65 years.

I cherish the memories of my long association with him, right from our days as Pracharaks of the RSS, to the inception of Bharatiya Jana Singh, the struggle of the dark months during the Emergency leading to the formation of Janata Party and later the emergence of the Bharatiya Janata Party in 1980.

Atalji will be remembered as the pioneer of the first ever stable non-Congress coalition government at the Centre and I had the privilege of working as his deputy for six years. As my senior, he always encouraged and guided me in every possible manner.

LK Advani, Veteran BJP leader

Today India lost a great son. Former PM Atal Bihari Vajpayeeji, was loved and respected by millions. My condolences to his family and all his admirers. We will miss him.

Rahul Gandhi, President, Indian National Congress

Vajpayee was a towering figure in our national life. Throughout his life, he stood for democratic values and demonstrated this commitment in all his acts, whether as a parliamentarian, a cabinet minister, or Prime Minister of India. He was a spell-binding orator, a leader of great vision, a patriot to the core for whom the national interest was paramount.

He was a man with a very large heart and a real spirit of magnanimity. One saw that in all his interactions - with other political parties and their leaders, with foreign governments, with coalition partners, and indeed with his own political colleagues, whom he always treated with respect and courtesy.

His warm personality and his gift of friendship won him admirers and friends across the political spectrum and from every walk of life. His death leaves behind a huge void.

Sonia Gandhi, Indian National Congress

The country has lost a true patriot who took great risks to build peace within the country and with our neighbours once he became the Prime Minister.

Mallikarjun Kharge, Congress leader in Lok Sabha

It is a great loss to the country. It was a joy to listen to Atalji, he cut across ideology, he was a person who had compassion and his belief to take India together is to be remembered. India has become poor in his loss. He has left a deep imprint.

Anand Sharma, Senior Congress leader

Vajpayeeji was a man of great wisdom, tolerance and compassion. He led his party to its first victory in national elections and established the credentials of the BJP to run the central government. He will be remembered for many things, but above all for his genuine efforts to resolve the decades-long hostility between Pakistan and India. As long as he was at the helm, he resolutely anchored the BJP close to the middle and did not allow the party to swing to the extreme right of the political spectrum. It is not the fact that Vajpayeeji had many friends, it is the fact that he had no enemies that was his distinguishing hallmark.

P Chidambaram, Senior Congress leader

With the sad demise of Bharatratna Atal Bihari Vajpayeeji, We have lost a great soul, an eloquent poet, orator par excellence, an excellent human being and one of the greatest Parliamentarians of India.

His passing away is a personal loss, having spent numerous years in our parliamentary life together, and an irreparable loss to our country. I pray eternal peace for his departed soul.

Sharad Pawar, President, Nationalist Congress Party

It was the speciality of Atalji that he never let humanity be harmed due to the political and ideological differences. Such principle is needed in the country today.

Sitaram Yechury, General Secretary, CPI(M)

Strong binding force of the National Democratic Alliance.

Pride, arrogance or rigidity of power was miles away from him; he was upright and honest, gentle and mild-mannered, and his perpetually smiling face an inspiration for all. I met him several times and he always blessed me like a father. Nobody can take his place.

Uddhav Thackeray, President, Shiv Sena

Extremely saddened to hear about the passing away of one of our greatest inspirations for nation building, Bharat Ratna Shri Atal Bihari Vajpayeeji. ॐ शांति शांति

Biplab Kumar Deb, Chief Minister, Tripura

He may be not with us physically but his vision will always be with us, losing a person whom we always looked up to is a personal loss for all of us and I am sure we will always take inspiration from his ideology.

Devendra Fadnavis, Chief Minister, Maharashtra

Very very saddened that the great statesman and former PM Shri Atal Bihari Vajpayeeji is no more with us. His passing away is a very big loss to our nation. I will always cherish the many fond memories. Condolences to his family and his many admirers.

Mamata Banerjee, Chief Minister, West Bengal

Deeply pained by the passing away of our beloved Atal ji. India has lost a great leader, a leader of masses and a visionary who dedicated his entire life in service of the nation and its people.

Manohar Parrikar, Chief Minister, Goa

The demise of Atal Bihari Vajpayee is not only a loss for the country, it is big loss for the people of Jammu and Kashmir. He was the first Prime Minister to understand the agony of our people.

Mehbooba Mufti, Former Chief Minister, J&K

I am deeply grieved at the sad demise of Vajpayeeji. India has lost one of its tallest leaders.

Naveen Patnaik, Chief Minister, Odisha

A poet, a statesman and a great leader passes away, leaving us desolate.

I'm saddened to hear the demise of former PM Shri Atal Bihari Vajpayeeji. I on behalf of the People of Manipur with tears in eyes and a heavy heart join millions in bidding a good bye. Your uniqueness shall live forever!

N Biren Singh, Chief Minister, Manipur

भारत के पूर्व प्रधानमंत्री एवं भारत रत्न अटल बिहारी वाजपेयी जी का निधन दुःखद। देश ने सबसे बड़े राजनीतिक शख्सियत, प्रखर वक्ता, लेखक, चिंतक, अभिभावक एवं करिश्माई व्यक्तित्व को खो दिया। उन्हें विनम्र श्रद्धांजलि।

India has lost the tallest political leader, a charismatic personality, poet, orator, writer and thinker.

Nitish Kumar, Chief Minister, Bihar

Vajpayee Sahib is no more and I feel a personal sense of loss at his passing. Thank you Sir for the opportunities, for the trust you reposed in me, for the opportunities to travel with you and to learn from you. You will be greatly missed.

Words mean so little at a time like this but words are all we have to convey the deepest condolences to Gunu, to Neha, to Ranjan and the entire family. May God give you strength to bear this tremendous loss.

Omar Abdullah, Former Chief Minister, J&K

Late Shri Atalji had the ability to bring harmony among all parties - ruling and opposition. This is visible from the way leaders from both sides of the aisle came together to pay tribute to the great soul.

Pema Khandu, Chief Minister, Arunachal Pradesh

आज मैंने अपने पिता तुल्य गुरु को खो दिया है। जीवन में कई ऐसे अवसर आए जब श्रद्धेय अटल बिहारी वाजपेयीजी का स्नेह और मार्गदर्शन प्राप्त करने का सौभाग्य मिला। युगपुरुष, भारतरत्न अटल जी को शत-शत नमन।

आदरणीय श्रद्धेय अटल बिहारी वाजपेयीजी के देहांत से मन बेहद विचलित है। भारतीय राजनीति में अटलजी का योगदान अविस्मरणीय रहेगा। अटलजी का सामाजिक जीवन अनंत काल तक आने वाली पीढ़ियों के लिए प्रेरणास्रोत बना रहेगा।

Raghubar Das, Chief Minister, Jharkhand

श्रद्धेय अटल बिहारी वाजपेयी जी ने गरीब कल्याण, ग्राम विकास के साथ नदी संरक्षण के जरिये समग्र विकास का जो मंत्र दिया, उसे आत्मसात कर हम लगातार आगे बढ़ रहे हैं। हम सब मिलकर उनके सपनों के सशक्त, खुशहाल और श्रेष्ठ भारत का निर्माण करेंगे, उनके प्रति यही सच्ची श्रद्धांजलि होगी।

Atalji's death is a great personal loss to me. I remember his words when I met him after I had lost my first election. He said, "Sarbananda, if you want to serve the people and society, you have to undergo challenges and sometimes even defeats in your life. But you must not feel disheartened or ever lose hope. You must concentrate only on serving the people and the country." I cannot explain how much strength and inspiration these words gave me. I will always cherish them.

Sarbananda Sonowal, Chief Minister, Assam

मैं परम श्रद्धेय अटल बिहारी वाजपेयीजी को अश्रुपूरित श्रद्धांजलि अर्पित करता हूं। हम सब के लिए ये दुखदायी क्षण है। हमारे सिर से पितृतुल्य ऐसे व्यक्तित्व का साया उठ गया, जिसने हमेशा चुनौतियों से लड़ने का साहस दिया, नई राह दिखाई। आज एक राजनीतिक युग का अंत हो गया।

जिनके शब्द हमारी शक्ति हैं, आशीर्वाद हमारी ऊर्जा, जिनकी प्रेरणा हमें देश सेवा के लिए समर्पित करे, ऐसे आदरणीय अटल बिहारी वाजपेयीजी के चरणों में बारंबार प्रणाम। ईश्वर दिवंगत आत्मा को शांति प्रदान करें।

श्रद्धेय अटल बिहारी वाजपेयीजी ने गरीब कल्याण, ग्राम विकास के साथ नदी संरक्षण के जरिये समग्र विकास का जो मंत्र दिया, उसे आत्मसात कर हम लगातार आगे बढ़ रहे हैं। हम सब मिलकर उनके सपनों के सशक्त, खुशहाल और श्रेष्ठ भारत का निर्माण करेंगे, उनके प्रति यही सच्ची श्रद्धांजलि होगी।

He was a great politician and loved by millions. It's unimaginable to think that our beloved Atal Ji is no more with us. This is an end of a political era, the void of his absence can never be filled.

Shivraj Singh Chouhan, Chief Minister, Madhya Pradesh

I remember those early days of BJP when under Atalji and Rajmataji I took my first steps into politics. Learning the ropes from the best, Atalji's wisdom and wit always proved to be an unmatched combination – his trademark style that India came to love.

With the passing of Shri Atal Bihari Vajpayeeji India has lost its tallest leader of modern times, a political thinker whose wit was unparalleled and a champion of India – even when the motherland was marred by the emergency and had lost all hope.

Vasundhara Raje, Chief Minister, Rajasthan

The demise of our beloved leader Vajpayee has created a void within us. He was a true national leader who followed the path of righteousness and served for the welfare of the country for more than five decades.

Without Vajpayee, India would not have been able to achieve the status of a nuclear power.

Vijay Rupani, Chief Minister, Gujarat

भारत की राजनीति में मूल्यों और आदर्शों को प्राथमिकता देने वाले, स्वतंत्र भारत के ढांचागत विकास के दूरदृष्टा, भारतीय राजनीति के शलाका पुरुष पूर्व प्रधानमंत्री श्रद्धेय अटल बिहारी वाजपेयीजी का निधन भारत की राजनीति के महायुग का अवसान है।

He worked in the national interest rather than personal interest, he brought a political stability to our country. His ashes will be spread in every river in UP to respect his grand stature.

Vajpayee always gave priority to values and ideals in politics.

Yogi Adityanath, Chief Minister, Uttar Pradesh

It is a big loss for the country, he was a very simple man inspite of being such a senior leader. There was not even a shred of arrogance in him. Current leaders need to learn a lot from him.

Mulayam Singh Yadav, Senior Samajwadi Party leader

Thank you Atal Bihari Vaajpayeeji for your LIFE and your LESSONS.

Anupam Kher

I'm saddened to hear the demise of a great statesman Shri Vajpayeeji. May his soul Rest In Peace.

Rajinikanth

All of us who knew Mr Atal Bihari Vajpayee are saddened to hear of his passing away. He was a great leader with a great sense of compassion and humour. He will be remembered fondly by a vast number of us.

Ratan Tata, Industrialist

The Indian Cricket Team and BCCI condoles the sad demise of former Prime Minister Shri Atal Bihari Vajpayee. Atalji dedicated his life in service of the nation.

Board of Control for Cricket in India (BCCI)

Foreign dignitaries who attended the cremation of Vajpayee, were: Bhutan's King Jigme Khesar Namgyal Wangchuk, Nepal's Foreign Minister Pradeep Kumar Gyawali, Sri Lanka's Acting Foreign Minister Lakshman Kiriella, Afghanistan's Deputy Foreign Minister Hekmat Khalil Karzai, Pakistan's Information Minister Syed Ali Zafar and Former Afghanistan President Hamid Karzai was also among the mourners.

Meanwhile, tributes continued to pour in for the leader widely credited with charting a new path in foreign policy for India in many areas, including a complete revamp of ties with the US and bringing India out of the nuclear closet.

Vajpayee in his address to the US Congress in 2000, had famously characterized US-India ties as a "natural partnership of shared endeavours." He recognized early on that the United States and India, based on their shared democratic values, could develop a partnership that would contribute to the economic prosperity and security of the region and the world.

Today, our two countries and our bilateral relationship continue to benefit from former Prime Minister Vajpayee's vision, which helped promote expanded cooperation.

Mike Pompeo, US Secretary of State

Atal Bihari Vajpayee rightly commanded great respect around the world. He will be remembered as a politician who made a major personal contribution to the friendly relations between our countries.

Vladimir Putin, President, Russia

Atal Bihari Vajpayee was one of India's great leaders – saddened by his passing and my thoughts are with his family and loved ones. He was a close partner of the UK. Those who remember his state visit to the UK in 2001 will know how well respected he was here.

Mark Fields, British Minister of State for Asia and the Pacific

Heartfelt condolences to the Government and people of India on the passing of Atal Bihari Vajpayee. The world will celebrate him as an exemplary statesman.

Tshering Tobgay, Prime Minister, Bhutan

Vajpayee was a visionary statesman with impeccable integrity and dedication, who will be remembered for his sagacity and exemplary selfless service to the people of India.

KP Sharma Oli, Prime Minister, Nepal

Today, we have lost a great humanist and a true friend of Sri Lanka. Former Prime Minister of India Atal Bihari Vajpayee was a visionary leader and an ardent defender of democracy. My condolences to his family and millions of his admirers around the world.

Mathripala Sirisena, President, Sri Lanka

I have had the privilege of knowing Shri AB Vajpayee since 1975. Furthermore, we had a close working relationship during my tenure are Prime Minister from 2001 to 2004. He played a vital role in ensuring stability in Sri Lanka.

Ranil Wickremesinghe, Prime Minister, Sri Lanka

I first met him in 1998 during the SAARC conference when all eyes were on Vajpayee and Sharif when the former pushed a glass of water towards Sharif and he lifted the glass and drank the water. They wanted to show each other that they are for friendship. In his heart, Vajpayee wanted peace in the region.

Lakshman Kiriella, Special Envoy, Sri Lanka

Shri Atal Bihari Vajpayee was our great friend and highly respected in Bangladesh. As a token of recognition for his invaluable contribution to our Liberation War in 1971, Bangladesh government conferred on him the Bangladesh Liberation War Honour. Today is certainly a day of great sadness for all of us in Bangladesh.

Sheikh Hasina, Prime Minister, Bangladesh

We remember him (Vajpayee) for his contribution to Bangladesh Liberation War and strong support to the people of Bangladesh. He had a great liking for Bengali music. I had the privilege of serving in Delhi as career diplomat when he became the Foreign Minister.

Abul Hassan Mahmood Ali, Foreign Minister, Bangladesh

He had a great smile. An example of his courtesy was when he walked me out to the door despite his knee surgery. He was a man of immense honour. It was a privilege to have worked with him.

A great son of India, a respected world statesman, a friend of Afghanistan. I had the honour of working with him over several meetings and engagements. I respected him deeply for his humility, for his wisdom, for his courteous behaviour to me and all those who visited India. The greatest element in him was his desire for peace and stability in the region for which he worked with dedication and selflessness. We mourn his loss.

Hamid Karzai, Former President, Afghanistan

Today, as India shines as a beacon of progress and development on the global stage, we cannot forget the strong and able stewardship of Vajpayee.

His was a leadership characterised by determination, perseverance, fairness and equity.

We were honoured to receive him in March 2000 as chief guest at the National Day celebrations and whenever he visited Mauritius.

Mauritius mourns the loss of a man who stood not only for India but also for Mauritius.

The Mauritius PM said the flags would fly at half-mast from sunrise to sunset at government buildings in the country. He also made an appeal to the private sector to do the same.

Pravind Kumar Jugnauth, Prime Minister, Mauritius

* * *

Mr Vajpayee, known as an avuncular politician, was credited with helping bring mainstream acceptance to his Hindu nationalist Bharatiya Janata Party (BJP).

The party had struggled for many years before gaining political prominence in the 1990s by carefully nurturing religious pride and projecting the Congress party as being softer on the country's Muslim minority group.

But later, it was Mr Vajpayee's personal charisma and moderate image that helped the BJP stitch together a broad-based coalition of smaller, disparate regional parties. Between 1999 and 2004, he deftly managed the unwieldy coalition government of fractious partners.

He deployed similar skills to begin a new peace process with his Pakistani counterpart, Nawaz Sharif, and traveled to Lahore in northeastern Pakistan by bus in February 1999. But the effort was undermined three months later when the Pakistani army and separatist militants launched an offensive in the Kargil mountains of Kashmir, a Himalayan region claimed by the two South Asian neighbors.

The Washington Post, Washington DC

India's Vajpayee, who set off nuke race and peace, has died.

Former Indian Prime Minister Atal Bihari Vajpayee, a Hindu nationalist who set off a nuclear arms race with rival Pakistan but later reached across the border to begin a groundbreaking peace process, died Thursday after a long illness. He was 93.

A onetime journalist, Vajpayee was in many ways a political contradiction: He was the moderate leader of an often-strident Hindu nationalist movement. He was a lifelong poet who revered nature but who oversaw India's growth into a swaggering regional economic power. He was the prime minister who ordered nuclear tests in 1998, stoking fears of atomic war between India and Pakistan. Then, a few years later, it was Vajpayee who made the first moves toward peace.

Associated Press, New York

Atal Bihari Vajpayee, who as India's Prime Minister from 1998 to 2004 stunned the world by ending a decades-old moratorium on nuclear weapons tests but nevertheless managed to ease tensions with Pakistan and build closer ties to the United States, died on Thursday in New Delhi. He was 93.

A published poet, Mr Vajpayee dabbled in law, journalism and rebellion against British colonialism as a young man. A leader of the Hindu nationalist opposition to the once-invincible Indian National Congress party of Gandhi and Nehru, he was virtually unknown outside India for most of his 50 years in politics.

The New York Times, New York

Three-time Indian Prime Minister Atal Bihari Vajpayee dies at 93, prompting Narendra Modi to pay tribute.

Vajpayee's supporters saw him as a skilled politician who managed to avoid fanaticism, a man who refused to see the world in black and white.

But his critics considered him the leader of a fanatic movement - a movement partially rooted in European fascism - that sought power by stoking public fears of India's large Muslim minority.

The one thing both sides could agree on was his honesty. Vajpayee was that rare thing in Indian politics: a man untainted by corruption scandals.

The South China Morning Post, Hong Kong

Vajpayee repeatedly met with Russian President Vladimir Putin during official visits and at international forums. In 2000, the two state leaders signed the Declaration on Strategic Partnership, which became the first document of this kind in relations between India and Russia.

TASS, Russian News Agency

Vajpayee, partisan of peace with Pakistan, dies.

Vajpayee was idolised in Pakistan as a sincere peacemaker

and wooed by rivals at home as the right man in the wrong party.

> "Suppose I am that - a nice man in the wrong party - what would you want me to do?"

Typical of how he ribbed his doting opponents, on this occasion, shortly before resigning from a 13-day stint as Prime Minister in May 1996. In 1998, he had another short innings, but which he packed with game-changing nuclear tests, and a landmark visit to Lahore by bus.

A glimpse of Vajpayee's diplomatic preferences can be seen from the fact that he favoured 'genuine non-alignment', an implied criticism of the movement founded by Jawaharlal Nehru. His pro-West politics was derived from the staunchly anti-Communist Rashtriya Swayamsevak Sangh (RSS), of which he was a lifelong member.

Dawn, Pakistan

Atal Bihari Vajpayee's tenure as Indian Prime Minister brought his country's emergence as a nuclear power, triggering fears of conflict with Pakistan....

A free marketeer by inclination, he was criticised by unions and civil servants for his policy of privatising some of India's government-owned corporations. But his support for new hi-tech industries made India a global IT player and fuelled the country's economic expansion. Like many Indian leaders before him, AB Vajpayee found himself having to hold together a sometimes fractious coalition to wield power.

But he was seen by many as a unifying force when divisions threatened Indian society and as a staunch defender of his country's borders.

BBC, London

Index